W9-CZV-589

CliffsNotes™

Going Online with AOL®

by Jennifer Kaufeld

IN THIS BOOK

- Find your way around the AOL interface.

- Send and receive electronic mail.

- Chat with friends or celebrities.

- Join in online discussions of topics that interest you.

- Reinforce what you learn with the CliffsNotes Review.

- Find more information about AOL and the Internet in the CliffsNotes Resource Center and online at www.cliffsnotes.com.

IDG Books Worldwide, Inc.
An International Data Group Company

Foster City, CA • Chicago, IL • Indianapolis, IN • New York, NY

IDG
BOOKS
WORLDWIDE

About the Author

Jennifer Kaufeld is the coauthor of America Online(r) For Dummies(r), Quick Reference. After being dragged kicking and screaming into the world of computers, she now spends her time reviewing educational software for home-schoolers and speaking on the educational use of computers and software.

Publisher's Acknowledgments

Editorial

Senior Project Editor: Kyle Looper

Acquisitions Editor: Andy Cummings

Copy Editor: William Barton

Technical Editors: Matt Converse, Matthew McClure

Production

York Production Services

IDG Books Indianapolis Production Department

CliffsNotes™ Going Online with AOL®

Published by

IDG Books Worldwide, Inc.

An International Data Group Company

919 E. Hillsdale Blvd.

Suite 400

Foster City, CA 94404

www.idgbooks.com (IDG Books Worldwide Web site)

www.cliffsnotes.com (Cliffs Notes Web site)

Note: If you purchased this book without a cover you should be aware that this book is stolen property. It was reported as "unsold and destroyed" to the publisher, and neither the author nor the publisher has received any payment for this "stripped book."

Copyright © 1999 IDG Books Worldwide, Inc. All rights reserved. No part of this book, including interior design, cover design, and icons, may be reproduced or transmitted in any form, by any means (electronic, photocopying, recording, or otherwise) without the prior written permission of the publisher.

Library of Congress Catalog Card No.: 99-64200

ISBN: 0-7645-8522-3

Printed in the United States of America

10 9 8 7 6 5 4 3 2 1

1O/SQ/QY/ZZ/IN

Distributed in the United States by IDG Books Worldwide, Inc.

Distributed by CDG Books Canada Inc. for Canada; by Transworld Publishers Limited in the United Kingdom; by IDG Norge Books for Norway; by IDG Sweden Books for Sweden; by IDG Books Australia Publishing Corporation Pty. Ltd. for Australia and New Zealand; by TransQuest Publishers Pte Ltd. for Singapore, Malaysia, Thailand, Indonesia, and Hong Kong; by Gotop Information Inc. for Taiwan; by ICG Muse, Inc. for Japan; by Norma Comunicaciones S.A. for Colombia; by Intersoft for South Africa; by Eyrolles for France; by International Thomson Publishing for Germany, Austria and Switzerland; by Distribuidora Cuspide for Argentina; by LR International for Brazil; by Ediciones ZETA S.C.R. Ltda. for Peru; by WS Computer Publishing Corporation, Inc., for the Philippines; by Contemporanea de Ediciones for Venezuela; by Express Computer Distributors for the Caribbean and West Indies; by Micronesia Media Distributor, Inc. for Micronesia; by Grupo Editorial Norma S.A. for Guatemala; by Chips Computadoras S.A. de C.V. for Mexico; by Editorial Norma de Panama S.A. for Panama; by American Bookshops for Finland. Authorized Sales Agent: Anthony Rudkin Associates for the Middle East and North Africa.

For general information on IDG Books Worldwide's books in the U.S., please call our Consumer Customer Service department at **800-762-2974**. For reseller information, including discounts and premium sales, please call our Reseller Customer Service department at **800-434-3422**.

For information on where to purchase IDG Books Worldwide's books outside the U.S., please contact our International Sales department at 317-596-5530 or fax **317-596-5692**.

For consumer information on foreign language translations, please contact our Customer Service department at **1-800-434-3422**, fax **317-596-5692**, or e-mail rights@idgbooks.com.

For information on licensing foreign or domestic rights, please phone **+1-650-655-3109**.

For sales inquiries and special prices for bulk quantities, please contact our Sales department at 650-655-3200 or write to the address above.

For information on using IDG Books Worldwide's books in the classroom or for ordering examination copies, please contact our Educational Sales department at **800-434-2086** or fax **317-596-5499**.

For press review copies, author interviews, or other publicity information, please contact our Public Relations department at **650-655-3000** or fax **650-655-3299**.

For authorization to photocopy items for corporate, personal, or educational use, please contact Copyright Clearance Center, 222 Rosewood Drive, Danvers, MA 01923, or fax **978-750-4470**.

LIMIT OF LIABILITY/DISCLAIMER OF WARRANTY: THE PUBLISHER AND AUTHOR HAVE USED THEIR BEST EFFORTS IN PREPARING THIS BOOK. THE PUBLISHER AND AUTHOR MAKE NO REPRESENTATIONS OR WARRANTIES WITH RESPECT TO THE ACCURACY OR COMPLETENESS OF THE CONTENTS OF THIS BOOK AND SPECIFICALLY DISCLAIM ANY IMPLIED WARRANTIES OF MERCHANTABILITY OR FITNESS FOR A PARTICULAR PURPOSE. THERE ARE NO WARRANTIES WHICH EXTEND BEYOND THE DESCRIPTIONS CONTAINED IN THIS PARAGRAPH. NO WARRANTY MAY BE CREATED OR EXTENDED BY SALES REPRESENTATIVES OR WRITTEN SALES MATERIALS. THE ACCURACY AND COMPLETENESS OF THE INFORMATION PROVIDED HEREIN AND THE OPINIONS STATED HEREIN ARE NOT GUARANTEED OR WARRANTED TO PRODUCE ANY PARTICULAR RESULTS, AND THE ADVICE AND STRATEGIES CONTAINED HEREIN MAY NOT BE SUITABLE FOR EVERY INDIVIDUAL. NEITHER THE PUBLISHER NOR AUTHOR SHALL BE LIABLE FOR ANY LOSS OF PROFIT OR ANY OTHER COMMERCIAL DAMAGES, INCLUDING BUT NOT LIMITED TO SPECIAL, INCIDENTAL, CONSEQUENTIAL, OR OTHER DAMAGES.

Trademarks: Cliffs, CliffsNotes, and all related logos and trade dress are registered trademarks or trademarks of Cliffs Notes, Inc. in the United States and other countries. AOL is a registered trademark of America Online, Inc. All other brand names and product names used in this book are trade names, service marks, trademarks, or registered trademarks of their respective owners. IDG Books Worldwide, Inc. and Cliffs Notes, Inc. are not associated with any product or vendor mentioned in this book.

is a registered trademark or trademark under exclusive license to IDG Books Worldwide, Inc. from International Data Group, Inc. in the United States and/or other countries.

IDG BOOKS WORLDWIDE

Table of Contents

INTRODUCTION

America Online is the largest online service in the world, boasting membership in excess of 20 million users. With so many people together, you may expect a lot of activity — and that's exactly what AOL delivers!

On America Online, you can send and receive e-mail, check out the latest news and weather, watch your stocks, plan a trip, participate in live chats with famous people, and much more. You can also participate in a plethora of AOL communities and interest groups covering a wide variety of topics. If that weren't enough, AOL is your springboard to the nearly endless collection of resources and information on the Internet.

Why Do You Need This Book?

Can you answer yes to any of these questions?

- Do you need to learn about AOL fast?
- Don't have time to read 500 pages about AOL?
- Do you want to get started with Internet e-mail right away?
- Do you need to find what you're looking for quickly?

If so, then CliffsNotes *Going Online with AOL* is for you!

How to Use This Book

You can read this book straight through or just look for the information you need. You can find information on a particular topic in a number of ways: You can search the index in the back of the book, locate your topic in the Table of

Contents, or read the In This Chapter list in each chapter. To reinforce your learning, check out the Review and the Resource Center at the back of the book. To help you find important information in the book, look for the following icons in the text:

This icon points out something worth keeping in mind.

This icon clues you in to helpful hints and advice.

This icon alerts you to something dangerous or to avoid.

Don't Miss Our Web Site

Keep up with the changing world of the Internet by visiting our Web site at www.cliffsnotes.com. Here's what you'll find:

- Interactive tools that are fun and informative
- Links to interesting Web sites
- Additional resources to help you continue your learning

At www.cliffsnotes.com you can even register for a new feature called CliffsNotes Daily, which offers you newsletters on a variety of topics, delivered right to your e-mail box each business day.

If you haven't yet discovered the Internet and are wondering how to get online, pick up *Getting On the Internet*, new from CliffsNotes. You'll learn just what you need to make your online connection quickly and easily. See you at www.cliffsnotes.com!

CHAPTER 1

A FIRST LOOK AT THE AMERICA ONLINE SCREEN

IN THIS CHAPTER

- Signing on to America Online
- Exploring Menu bar options
- Using Toolbar tricks

Before taking off for the far-reaching depths of America Online and cyberspace, you want to become familiar with the various buttons, boxes, and other gadgets you come across while you're online. You can spend hours clicking everything in sight just to see what it does, but going forth with a plan in mind may prove easier (and less stressful to your mouse-clicking fingers). This chapter helps you through the sign-on/sign-off process and then gives you a basic overview of the windows and buttons on the America Online screen.

Getting On and Off the System

Face it: Connecting to the world through your modem, phone line, and computer is just plain *fun*. Researching topics of interest, finding new people with whom to connect, or even just poking around to see what's out there in cyberspace occupies many of you for hours at a time. First, however, you need to know how to get into (and out of) America Online.

Signing on

You'll probably find the America Online software already installed on your system — especially if you have a relatively new computer. If you don't see the blue-green America Online triangle icon on your desktop and you missed getting a copy in the mail (seems like those CD-ROMs are everywhere these days), then you can get a free CD-ROM and 50 hours of free service sent to you by dialing 1-800-827-3338 (for international calls, dial +1-703-264-1184).

To begin your online adventures, you first need to sign on to America Online. To do so, just follow these steps:

1. Start the America Online software by double-clicking the America Online icon on your desktop. The Sign On dialog box appears, patiently awaiting your password, as shown in Figure 1-1.

2. If you use more than one screen name (your online nickname), select the screen name that you want to use from the Select Screen Name list. To open the list and select a name, click the down arrow in the Select Screen Name list box and then click the screen name from the list.

3. Click the Enter Password text box and type your password.

4. Take a second to make sure that your modem is on (if you have an external modem) and that no one else is on the phone. Then click Sign On. America Online shows you a set of three graphics while it connects to the service and checks your password. After the Welcome screen appears, you're signed on and ready to go!

If the system rejects your password, you probably mistyped a letter or number. Carefully retype your password into the Invalid Password, Please Re-enter dialog box that appears and then click OK.

Figure 1-1:   The Sign On window awaits your secret password.

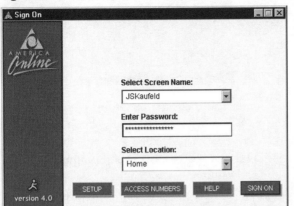

Every so often, the connection to America Online doesn't quite go through. If that happens, click Cancel and try again. If the connection still doesn't work, wait a few moments and try once or twice more before giving in and calling America Online technical support (at 1-800-827-3338).

Signing off

After you finish cruising the online world, sign off the service and shut down the software. Closing the software frees up your computer's resources to do other things. You can sign off AOL in either of the following ways:

■ Sign off the system by choosing Sign Off⇨Sign Off. Then choose File⇨Exit to close the program.

■ To sign off and close the program in one step, either choose File⇨Exit or (for Windows 95/98 users) click the Close box in the upper-right corner of the screen.

If you forget to sign off before wandering away from the computer to fix a cup of tea, America Online signs you off automatically after ten minutes or so. After you return to the computer, you see AOL's sign-off window on-screen with the following terse message: `Your account has been logged off due to inactivity. Please call back soon.`

Peering into the Welcome Window

After you connect to the America Online computers, you hear a hearty "Welcome" as the Welcome screen appears (see Figure 1-2). Think of the Welcome screen as your first peek into America Online — as well as a good jumping-off point for an online adventure.

Figure 1-2: Welcome to America Online!

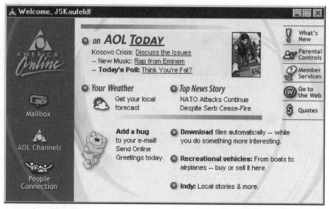

Here AOL provides you with links to many informative places online. Read the latest news story, check the weather, or see who sent you mail — each with just a click of the mouse.

In the Welcome window — as well as anyplace else on America Online — you activate things by clicking your mouse. Any time the mouse pointer turns into a hand, consider it fair game for a click. Most of the time, a click in the Welcome window opens yet another window full of information.

The following list describes the handy windows you can access from the Welcome screen:

- **What's New** (keyword: **New**) in the top-right corner of the Welcome window takes you to a screen touting the latest and greatest on AOL. From this window, you can find out what the currently featured areas (such as Computing or Moms Online) offer that's new and different. This screen also leads to the newest areas on America Online. Pick a topic that looks interesting and try one. Many times, these areas lead to America Online windows, but some of them may open your Web browser and take you to a Web site.

- **Parental Controls** (keyword: **Parental Controls**) takes you to an area that enables you to create a new screen name especially for the younger set — with restricted access to the Internet and online functions such as electronic mail, if you so choose. You can find out more about Parental Controls and screen names in Chapter 2.

- **Member Services** (keyword: **Help**) gives tips for new members, basic instruction in using features such as electronic mail or the Internet, and information on AOL's various billing options.

- **Go to the Web** opens America Online's Web browser and takes you directly to AOL.com, America Online's own Web page. Select one of the featured categories, such as Mortgage Calculators, TV Listings, or Personal Finance, to learn about Internet-based resources on these topics and, seemingly, a hundred others.

- **Quotes** (keyword: **Quotes**) opens America Online's stock quotes window. Want to know how that stock's been doing before you sink any money into it? Open this window, enter the company's trading symbol into the text box, and click Get Quote. Use the Name radio button in the Quotes window to see a company's symbol if you don't already know it by heart.

Although America Online provides recent quotes, these figures certainly aren't what you'd consider "real-time" information — changes coming to you the second they happen. Because you experience about a 25-minute delay before the information hits America Online's system (and your computer screen), basing any heavy trading or financially changing decisions on the information you glean here isn't wise. The market moves way too fast to try any heavy trading with a 25-minute delay.

■ **The Mailbox** changes to a box with a yellow letter sticking out and `You Have Mail` written underneath after a message lands in your electronic mailbox. To read your mail, click the full mailbox icon. If you have no waiting mail, clicking the mailbox takes you to the AOL Mail Center, an area full of helpful tips and suggestions for using e-mail.

■ **AOL Channels** moves the Channels window to the forefront. The Channels generally spend their time hiding behind the Welcome window on-screen. From this window, you can explore America Online's content by topic. Whether your interests lie in cars, computing, or collectibles you can find the topic you seek somewhere under an AOL Channel.

■ **People Connection** (keyword: **People Connection**) takes you to AOL's chat feature, where you can choose a chat by subject or simply drop into a random chat room and join the conversation.

■ **On AOL Today** (keyword: **AOL Today**) gives you a screen with up-to-date news stories, interesting features, a listing of the evening's television programming, business and market news, and job search information. Plus look here for daily online special guests or shopping deals.

■ **Your Weather** gives you a daily overview for the entire United States and for your local area; or you can type the name of any city in the text box and click Search for an expanded forecast for that area of the country. Use the World Weather button in the window to check thunderstorms in Thailand or breezes in Bangladesh.

■ **Top News Story** opens the news window, complete with top stories, daily features, and a news ticker.

Look in the bottom center of the Welcome window for changing features. This section of the window offers items for purchase online, a tip or two to make online life easier, and a link to your city's local online area.

Choosing a Channel

For a topical overview of America Online, turn to the *Channels window*. You can find it by clicking the *AOL Channels button* on the Welcome window, by using the keyword **Channels**, or by clicking the window that's half hidden behind the Welcome screen. Any way that you get there, the Channels window appears on-screen, ready to lead you into the depth of America Online.

America Online divides its online content into 19 channels, plus a search engine that the service calls *Find*. From Games to Health to Research & Learn, America Online covers nearly every area of interest under these channels, which are topical windows containing links to various other online areas. Each channel also contains a Search & Explore button that lists the contents of that particular channel.

Using the Menu Bar

The *menu bar* at the top of the screen gives you one way to communicate with the America Online software (see Figure 1-3). Here's where you turn if you're looking for commands such as "please rearrange all those windows so that I can see what I'm doing" or "I need a spell checker now!"

Figure 1-3: Use the menu bar to access editing commands and to arrange windows.

File Edit Window Sign Off Help

The menu bar presents you with five choices, and each one functions as a pull-down menu. Click the name of any item in the menu bar to see the organizational treasures that it conceals, as the following list describes:

■ **File:** Covers printing and saving information and opens files already stored on your hard drive.

■ **Edit:** If you need a dictionary, thesaurus, or spell checker, look for them here. Edit also contains the text-editing commands cut, copy, and paste.

■ **Window:** This menu helps you arrange the windows on-screen. It also features a list of open windows at the bottom of the screen. Use this menu whenever you want to visit a window that you still have open on-screen, but is buried somewhere down at the bottom of the pile. This menu's Cascade item also comes in handy — it arranges all the open windows so that you can click on any window and bring it to the top of the stack.

■ **Sign Off:** Use this menu to switch screen names or sign off the system after you finish exploring online.

■ **Help:** If you need access to Parental Controls, Member Services Online Help, or Accounts and Billing information, turn to the Help menu.

Clicking the Toolbar Buttons

Stretched across the top of the screen, from one side to the other, the *toolbar buttons* sparkle with color and small images (better known as *icons*), as shown in Figure 1-4. In addition to its colorful display, the toolbar works hard to make your online visits easy. Most of the buttons show a little *downward-pointing triangle* next to the icon. These buttons open a drop-down list after you click them and work much like the menu-bar items. Click a button and slide the mouse pointer down the list, highlighting choices until you find something interesting. Release the mouse button after you find an area you want to visit, and that window opens on-screen.

Figure 1-4:   Bright and colorful, the toolbar reveals online treasures.

Buttons with no triangles act as shortcuts, directly opening an online area or dialog box after you click them. After you get used to them, toolbar buttons save you considerable time trying to find certain areas and online features, as the following list describes:

- **Read:** Opens your screen name's mail window, showing all new mail.

- **Write:** Opens the Write Mail window so that you can compose an e-mail message.

- **Mail Center:** This drop-down list lets you open your e-mail Address Book, read old mail (messages you've already read before), and Run an Automatic AOL session.

- **Print:** Print whatever text appears in the current window.

- **My Files:** Open the Download Manager, your Personal Filing Cabinet, and the Log Manager from a drop-down list.

- **My AOL:** Use this drop-down list to customize America Online to some extent. Change or delete Screen Names, open your Member Profile, change your Password, and set Parental Controls, all from this button's listings.

■ **Favorites:** Opens the Favorite Places window or the Keyword dialog box. Also use this drop-down list to see your top Favorite Places as well as online areas that AOL considers "must sees."

■ **Internet:** Look for phone numbers through the Internet White Pages or Internet Yellow Pages, open the Web browser, or go to AOL Netfind to search for items on the Web.

■ **Channels:** Select one of the channels from this drop-down list and go directly there.

■ **People:** Find a chat room where you can laugh and talk with other members online, open the Instant Message window, or check the online guest appearances list in AOL Live. Select your choice from the drop-down list that appears.

■ **Quotes:** Check on the progress of your favorite stocks.

■ **Perks:** Take a peek at moneysaving offers available to AOL members.

■ **Weather:** Open the Weather window so that you can check the day's highs and lows.

■ **AOL Icon:** This icon flashes and spins to show you that the software is working hard. Click any button and you get to watch it dance. (Clicking the icon itself, however, does absolutely nothing.)

If your screen doesn't show the Quotes, Perks, and Weather buttons, don't panic. This merely means that your screen is set to a 640 x 480 resolution, so the buttons don't fit on your screen. Depending on the age of the computer system and the size of your monitor screen, you may be able to set the resolution higher (as in 800 x 600). On the other hand, maybe you can't — but in either case, both America Online and the AOL software are fine, whether or not you see those last three buttons.

Browser Bar

The *browser bar* hangs out right underneath the toolbar on-screen (see Figure 1-5). This small, thin strip may well become your favorite feature of the America Online 4.0 software. In addition to helping you access the Internet, the browser bar also excels at general online navigation — its text box keeps a running tab of where you've been, which is a supreme help if you want to revisit that window from an hour ago and have no idea where to find it. The browser bar puts the following features at your (mouse's) fingertips:

Figure 1-5:   Hop onto the browser bar and take a spin on the Web.

- **Previous:** This backward-pointing arrow takes you to the last window you visited. Keep clicking it to go back-ward, window by window.

- **Next:** Use this forward-pointing arrow to revisit windows you've already seen online. Next only operates after you've used the Previous button.

- **Stop:** Clicking this circular icon containing the little *X* stops the Web browser from loading the current page. Use this button if you change your mind or find the page taking too long to load.

- **Refresh:** Click this circular arrow button to reload the current Web page if something appears wrong with the page. (Sometimes Web-site graphics don't load right, or you find the page missing huge parts of text.) Refresh reloads the page and starts over. If Refresh doesn't fix the problem, chalk it up to a flaky Web site and move on — it's not a problem with the AOL software.

- **Home:** This house-shaped button opens your home Web page. Generally, clicking this button loads AOL.com into your Web browser.

■ **Find:** Clicking Find starts the system's AOL Find service or AOL's Web search Netfind.

■ **Text box:** Enter a keyword or a Web address and then click the Go button to open that area or Internet site.

■ **Arrow:** Click this downward-pointing triangle immediately to the right of the text box to view a list of the online areas and Web pages you've visited during your online session.

■ **Go:** Go to the area or Internet site that's currently in the text box.

■ **Keyword:** This button opens the keyword dialog box so that you can enter keywords there instead of needing to use the browser bar's text box.

Hover the mouse pointer over the browser bar buttons without clicking to identify each button's function.

CHAPTER 2

CHANNELS – AOL'S TOPICAL OVERVIEW

IN THIS CHAPTER

- Selecting a channel from the Channels window.
- Using the channels as a topical guide to AOL
- Playing games in the Games channel

Travelers have two ways to get where they're going. Either they go directly from one destination to another, without so much as stopping for an extended petrol break, or they meander from small town to small town, stopping at intriguing shops and points of interest along the way.

As an America Online member, you, too, have options. Choosing to go directly to a point of interest via an AOL keyword is one way to get where you're going. An equally valid method is to leisurely cruise through the various *channels* in the Channels window.

This chapter gives you a basic overview of what you find in each channel. To unearth the real treasures, however, you want to delve further into your favorite channels to see what catches your eye.

Viewing the Channels Window

The AOL *Channels window* lies right behind the Welcome window as you sign on, and organizes AOL's forums and online areas into large topical windows. You can also access it by clicking the Channels button on the Welcome window itself. The Channels window opens for your perusal 19 online worlds ready for exploration (see Figure 2-1). Because each channel's topic is so broad, however, the trick is in finding exactly what you're looking for.

Figure 2-1: So many channels — so little time.

Turn to Chapter 5 for more information about *keywords*, the direct route to online destinations.

Find

First on the list of Channel window buttons, the Find system plays a prominent role in online life. Not really a channel per se, *Find* opens the AOL Search window and enables you to search through the online jungle for those topics that interest you. In addition to a text box in which you type the word(s) you want AOL to search for, the window offers links to other resources such as Online Events, AOL Netfind (a Web-searching system), Software, and Products. (See Chapter 6 for more information about AOL NetFind.)

AOL Today

Designed around the day's news, activities, and events, *AOL Today* brings you various types of content depending on the time of day you visit (see Figure 2-2). Here you can read news stories, check out David Letterman's Top Ten List, answer a daily poll question, find a new recipe for dinner, or discover a new video to rent, all within the confines of this one channel.

Figure 2-2:   AOL Today brings you current news and special offers.

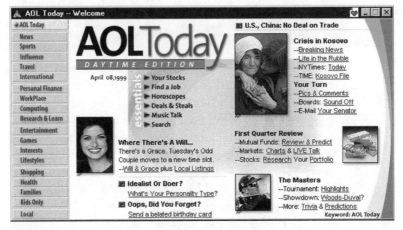

Tip

Because AOL Today draws from the entire service, it's a good channel to keep in mind if you want to learn more about America Online. From this one window, you could visit news windows, music and entertainment information, hobby areas, and various shopping vendors throughout the day.

News

Whatever news you want to read, the *News* channel offers it. Its eight departments focus on news from the U.S., World, Business, and Sports, as well as Politics, Life, Weather, Local news, and Classifieds.

The News channel offers plenty of convenient features, too. Watch the news ticker flash the current hour's headlines and click a headline if you want to know more. Take a daily news poll on some burning issue. Click the TIME.com button for information on the day's scheduled live event, where some notable newsmaker (or news follower) appears in one of the large online chat auditoriums, discusses the current news, and often takes questions from AOL members in the "audience." After reading the News channel contents for a few days, you're bound to feel incredibly current.

Sports

Balls. Bats. Pucks. Scores. Uniforms. Trades. Wheels. If these terms thrill your heart and make you want to grab the remote (or your baseball mitt), then turn to the *Sports* channel to meet your competitive needs. This window lists everything from golf to extreme sports, and each button leads you to a screen full of information, statistics, news, messages, and scores for that particular sport. If you thought you were the only person in the world who follows baton twirling, darts, or paintball, look no further. The Sports channel contains forums devoted to these sports and much, much more. (Click the More Sports button to find anything that the main window doesn't list.)

Influence

Whenever you see the *Influence* channel, think "Society Page." Dedicated to celebrity stories, fashion updates, and the media, this channel explores popular opinion and the latest trends in everything from financial savvy to gourmet cooking. Each of the Influence channel's five departments addresses a different interest. Turn to the Seen & Heard department for celebrity news; The Good Life department for travel, fashion, and dining out tips; and the Arts &

Leisure department for information on the latest in culture and the newest books. The Media & Money department discusses finance and news, and The Inner Circle department takes you to online Influence chat and message boards.

Travel

Before you head out on that next vacation or business trip, take a look at the *Travel* channel. Offering vacation tips, online reservations, and destination ideas, Travel provides more ideas for your next trip than you can possibly use in a lifetime of yearly vacations. For topical travel ideas, such as family travel or an adventure trip, click the Travel Interests department button.

International

Visit the *International* channel to silence that longing for world travel. (On the other hand, a trip to International may simply encourage you to save for that big vacation.) Click the world map to explore the globe continent by continent or use the department list to open windows focusing on international games, global business news, international travel information, or cultural exploration.

As the mouse hovers over various continents of the map, look for pop-up boxes containing country names beginning with "AOL," such as AOL France, which denote America Online's international services. Clicking the world map's button over Europe, for example, opens a window with a map sporting buttons for AOL UK, AOL France, AOL Sweden, AOL Austria, AOL Germany, and AOL Switzerland. Clicking any of these buttons actually takes you to the international version of the America Online software.

Personal Finance

Keep track of dollars and dimes with help from the *Personal Finance* channel. Dedicated to information and chatter about investments, stocks, business, and taxes, Personal Finance offers tips, scheduled online chats, message boards, and — of course — an opportunity to trade online.

If you're new to investing and personal finance, begin with the Investing Basics department, which offers general, beginning information on investments — plus a large number of additional resources in the department window's item list that you may want to read.

Although they may offer some good tips, many of the investment areas online are sponsored by financial companies that would love to do business with you. Lying to you obviously isn't in their best interests, but watch out for slants on the truth as you deal with them or read their information. Remember — they're in business to make money, not only to help you learn about investing.

WorkPlace

Whether you work for a living, you find the idea of running a home business appealing, or you want to connect with others in the profession you're about to join (or just left), the *WorkPlace* channel has something for your interests (see Figure 2-3). WorkPlace provides information for people who want to change professions as well as support for those who love what they do. Chock-full of resources, tips, and job-search help, WorkPlace offers everything from business building assistance to a place to find that dream job. Denizens who hang out here discuss the ups and downs of their jobs, share thoughts on special work situations and their accompanying challenges, and sometimes just visit and relax.

Figure 2-3:   Whether you love work or hate it, WorkPlace contains plenty of stuff for you.

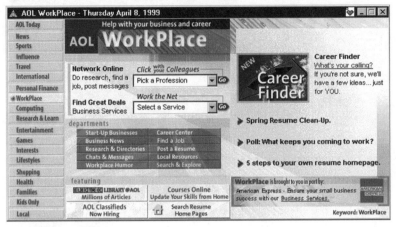

Computing

What would an online service be without a section on computers? The *Computing* channel features information for most computer users, whether you call your system a Macintosh, DOS, or Windows machine. From the main channel window, you can visit the Online Classroom and take a free computer course or two. The Help Desk department offers tips and assistance on all kinds of computer topics. Check out the Building Home Pages department to learn how to create your own Web page with a little help from America Online. And don't miss the Download Software department, which contains more downloadable shareware than a normal hard drive could possibly hold.

Research & Learn

The *Research & Learn* channel contains resources for the learner in you (or the student in your household). This window contains links to encyclopedias, dictionaries, phone books, foreign-language dictionaries, and quotations. Look here, too, for assistance in subject areas such as history, science, health, or writing. If you're in need of a science-fair project, check the Science department's project list. If a student in your household has difficulty with a school assignment, use Research & Learn's Ask a Teacher area to locate the answer.

Entertainment

Tune into the *Entertainment* channel for the latest scoop on entertainment news, television, celebrity stuff, and other Tinseltown trivia. Want to know about the latest home video or that upcoming movie? The Entertainment channel generally holds the reviews and release information you need. You can use the Books department to read up on current bestsellers and other books worth reading, while a trip into the Music department catches you up with the latest releases for nearly any type of music, from classical to rap.

Games

Relax, meet new online friends, and just have fun in the *Games* channel. Whether your taste runs to crossword puzzles, card games, strategy games, or fantasy role playing, you can find something to satisfy you here. Some of the games even enable you to play live against other AOL players.

America Online classifies many of the games in this channel as *Premium Games*. This classification means that AOL charges you a fee to play them — in addition to your regular monthly America Online access fee. Most of the strategy games, classic card games, and adventure games fall into the Premium Games category. Currently, AOL offers two different fee structures: For $0.99 per hour, you can play Game Parlor games such as Bridge, Blackjack, Chess, or Virtual Pool. Role-playing and adventure games, such as *MultiPlayer BattleTech Solaris*, *Air Warrior III*, or *Warcraft II* cost $1.99 per hour.

AOL's Game Shows section contains puzzle games, trivia games, and word games that the regular America Online fee covers. Check there if you want to play games for free.

Interests

Research a new recipe. Meet fellow members who love cars. Swap stories about your favorite pet. The *Interests* channel covers content galore — from a huge Hobbies area to a department devoted to photography buffs (see Figure 2-4). Its six main departments , called Auto Center, Food, Home & Garden, Hobbies, Pets, and Pictures, cover most leisure topics outside of Sports or Computing (which have their own online channels). If you want to connect with someone who shares your passion or find a new hobby to round out your collection, turn to Interests.

Figure 2-4:   Pick a passion — any passion — in the Interests channel.

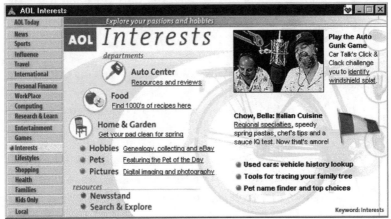

Lifestyles

The *Lifestyles* channel devotes its time to investigating the things that are truly important in life. Whether your interests lie in Self Improvement, Spirituality, Romance, or one of the Ages & Stages of life, turn to Lifestyles to help you expand your horizons. Divided into departments such as Teens, Ethnicity, and Women, Lifestyles explores the strengths of diverse lifestyle values and helps build community bonds among AOL members by helping them rally around the beliefs and lifestyles for which they live.

Shopping

What do you want to buy today? No matter what you need, the *Shopping* channel probably carries it. From fashions to flowers and from gourmet foods to gifts, Shopping offers the equivalent of a huge mall's contents.

Boasting 16 departments, beginning with Apparel and ending with Toys, Shopping saves wear and tear on your car while it gives your Visa card a workout. America Online's satisfaction guarantee covers all merchandise that you purchase from the Shopping channel; you can read about this guarantee by clicking the Customer Service button on the main Shopping window.

Health

Explore the *Health* channel and learn what you can do to increase your own healthy lifestyle. If you need a support group, have questions about various maladies, or want to move to a more active lifestyle, the Health channel appears, fully prepared — with online discussion groups, information, and shopping opportunities.

No matter where you fall on the health continuum, you can find assistance in one of the channel's nine departments: Illnesses & Treatments, Healthy Living, Support Groups & Experts, Medical Reference, Online Pharmacy, Women, Men, Children, and Seniors.

Families

Families have found a lot of support from America Online since the beginning of the service, and the *Families* channel groups AOL's online parenting resources all together. From Pregnancy all the way through High School, look for willing ears, helpful articles, and fun activities from this channel.

Whether you're facing a child's "stage" or hunting for entertainment options for the weekend, the Families channel helps maintain your sanity while providing you a place to dialog with other parents who've already been there.

Kids Only

So far, most of these online areas are geared to adults — or at least to teens and older. Never fear, however; in the *Kids Only* channel, the youngsters find a place of their own to congregate and follow their interests (see Figure 2-5). Kids Only is designed to be a safe place for children ages six through 12 to explore the online world. It offers news, sports, art activities, online clubs, games, and homework help.

Parents can limit children's online access so that they can visit Kids Only and nowhere else online. Use keyword: **Parental Controls** to find out how. The Kids Only channel is staffed by a group of adults whose main responsibility is to keep the kids safe while providing a fun (and educational) time for them online.

Figure 2-5:   The Kids Only channel gives kids a place to hang out online.

Local

Visit the *Local* channel to feel as though you dropped into one of the nation's larger cities for a tour. With a mix of local flavor and tourist tips for each city, the Local channel fills two functions at once: First, it's an area to scour if you're thinking of visiting a particular locale; second, you can also look at Local as a place to hang out and meet people if you happen to be a resident of one of its featured cities.

To see what treasures lie in store for a particular city, click the button that lies closest to its name on the map. That city's local window opens, showing news, local sports scores, entertainment options, travel tips, and residents' opinions on everything from the best dining-out experience to proposed zoning changes.

CHAPTER 3

BUILDING AN ONLINE IDENTITY

IN THIS CHAPTER

- Creating a screen name or two
- Deleting screen names
- Using screen names to set parental controls
- Creating an online profile

Imagine describing a friend to someone you've never met before. What terms would you use? Could you describe your friend by using her name, hobbies, occupation, or lifestyle? How about height, weight, hair color, or eye color? Which words convey the person's essence to someone totally new?

Although windows throughout AOL sport icons, graphics, and pictures galore, *words* are your greatest tool in communicating with other members online. By using words, you can create a pretend identity for an online role-play in the Games channel, for example; you can also project what's important to you through your screen name or tell others about yourself through an online profile. Depending on your interests (and how many family members share your account), you can even do all three.

This chapter gives you ideas for creating an AOL identity and helps you explain yourself to the many people online who probably are going to know you only through the word picture that you paint.

Screen Names Tell a Little . . . or a Lot

Think of an America Online screen name as the first glimpse others get of who you are. A screen name such as "HmTeacher" tells a whole lot more about somebody than "Steve98998" or " B123456789." Face it — who'd you rather talk to, HmTeacher or the B-number?

Some people use several screen names. You can use one screen name for work, for example, and another for free time. If you like adventure or role-playing games, where you interact live with other members, you need a special screen name for play as well. Base your screen names on your comfort level — how much you're comfortable with others online knowing about you.

If you want people to know more about you, create a name that contains your name or a particular interest — especially if a main reason for joining the online world is to meet others with similar interests. If you consider yourself a private person and want people to know as little about you as possible until you reveal more, a screen name such as "Cat4567890" may fit you. Keep in mind, however, that people sending and receiving electronic mail must use your screen name as your mailing address. If the idea of receiving mail to "Cat4567890" bothers you, choose a more specific screen name.

Each America Online account has space for up to five screen names. The first one that you create at the time you sign up for AOL is known as a *master screen name;* anyone using this screen name has full access to the service and can create or delete other screen names on the account. You can place various limitations on the other screen names you create, known in AOL as Parental Controls.

Creating a Screen Name

Give creativity full reign whenever you create a new screen name for yourself or a family member. When you create a new screen name, AOL allows you to specify whether you want it to be a *master screen name,* which is capable of setting controls on other screen names in the account, or a *general screen name* with either adult (general) or limited access. Master screen names also have the capability to change billing options with America Online.

You can have a maximum of only five screen names per account. If screen name creation hits you in a big way and you find at some point that you already have five screen names, you need to delete one of them before you can create a new one.

To create a screen name, follow these steps:

1. Sign on to America Online using your master screen name.

2. Use the keyword **Screen Names** or click the My AOL button from the button bar and select Screen Names from the list that appears to open the Create or Delete a Screen Name dialog box.

3. Double-click Create a Screen Name in the item list. The Create a Screen Name dialog box appears (see Figure 3-1). Click the Create Screen Name button in the new window to continue.

Figure 3-1: Let your imagination soar in creating a new screen name.

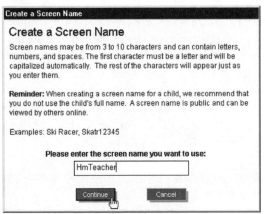

> **4.** Type the new screen name into the text box of the Create a Screen Name dialog box and then press Enter. If that name's already taken, AOL suggests another one — generally AOL helpfully tacks numbers to the end of whatever screen name you created so that it becomes a unique name. Either accept AOL's suggestion or try again with a new screen name.
>
> **5.** Type a password for the new screen name into the Set Password dialog box that appears. Then press Tab, retype the password, and press Enter. The Parental Controls dialog box appears on-screen.
>
> **6.** Select the age range (which represents the degree of access that you want) for the person using the screen name and click Continue. America Online automatically places Parental Controls on that screen name if you select an age range here. This way, you can specify that younger users have access to less of the service and the Internet than older children. (See the following section for more information on Parental Controls.)
>
> If you select General Access (18+), AOL asks whether you want the new screen name to function with Master Screen Name powers. If you don't want the person using this screen name to have the capability of changing

billing options or altering Parental Controls on the other names in the account, select the No radio button. Click the Continue button.

7. Click Accept Settings in the Your New Screen Name dialog box that appears to make your changes final.

Congratulations! You're finished. America Online creates the screen name and adds it to your software.

AOL requires that all new screen names comply with their Terms of Service Agreement. In other words, the screen name must be tasteful and clean — AOL doesn't permit offensive or vulgar screen names. If you create an unacceptable screen name and another member reports it as a screen-name violation, the America Online cops take a look. Then they kill your screen name if they agree. Gone. Poof. Nada.

Parental Controls

America Online gives you the opportunity to set limits on any youngsters who use your account. Like any large group of 17 million people, America Online (as well as the Internet) contains some places that you probably don't want to visit. Use Parental Controls when creating a new screen name for the kids to keep them out of places they're too young to see.

Whenever you create a new screen name for a child or teen, you determine what level of control you want to exert over the child's account. If you later find that the level you set is either too restrictive for your particular child or not restrictive enough, you can change it through the Parental Controls window (see Figure 3-2). You can access that window by clicking the My AOL button on the button bar and selecting Parental Controls from the list that appears. Click the Set Parental Controls Now button to open a window where you can change the overall level of control for any screen name except the master screen name.

Figure 3-2: You can change a screen name's level of access in the Parental Controls window.

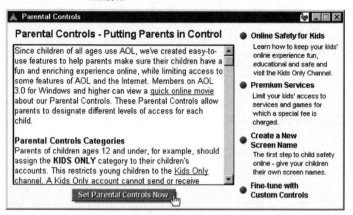

Divided into the following four categories and designed and maintained by the America Online staff, Parental Controls become less restrictive as the age levels rise:

- **Kids Only:** Designed for ages six through 12, the Kids Only controls limit the little Net surfers to the Kids Only channel on AOL and to child-appropriate Web sites. Kids Only controls give no access to most chat rooms or Instant Messages, and they block all attached files from e-mail messages.

- **Young Teen:** For 13- through 15-year-olds, Young Teen provides access to Web sites appropriate for that age group. This control level blocks access to chat rooms created by members, Instant Messages, and files attached to e-mail messages.

- **Mature Teen:** Designed for 16- and 17-year-olds, this Parental Control blocks Web sites deemed inappropriate for older teens.

- **General Access:** For adults ages 18 and older, this level gives the user access to the entire America Online service and the Internet.

Although the Parental Controls are a good thing, they're no substitute for parental supervision. Depending on your views and the particular child's maturity level, you might find the kids accessing some areas you don't want them to visit — even with the controls in place. Take the time to find out how your children use AOL and where they go while online. Personal involvement beats mechanical controls every time.

AOL automatically blocks all screen names except the master screen name from playing Premium Games. To remove the block, sign on with the master account and use keyword **Parental Controls.** Click the Premium Services button and then click in the check boxes to deselect screen names of any user who you want to have access to Premium Games.

Passwords

Your password keeps your account safe. If someone knows your password, that person can sign on to your account, send e-mail pretending to be you, create a new screen name for himself, and generally wreak havoc at your expense.

Avoid trouble and heartache by keeping your password under wraps. Don't tell *anyone* — and just to be safe, you may want to change your password every month or two. A good password consists of both letters and numbers, and it uses at least six characters. In fact, the America Online software refuses to accept any password with fewer than six characters.

Stay away from common numbers or words such as a pet's name, birth date, anniversary dates, social-security numbers, or any other word or number common to your life. If you must use a word that you like, translate it into a different language for use as your password. "Merlin," for example, may be a pretty easy password for someone to guess if friends know of your interest in the tales of King Arthur . . . but not if you type it in Welsh!

To change your password, use the keyword **Password** to open the Change Your AOL Password dialog box and click the Change Password button to open the Change Your Password dialog box (see Figure 3-3). Then enter your old password once and your new password twice into the text boxes. Click Change Password again to make it real.

Figure 3-3:   Remember to write down that new password somewhere safe.

Deleting Screen Names

The time may come to say goodbye to one or more of your screen names. America Online lets you delete any of the four secondary screen names from your account. You can't delete the master screen name (the first screen name that you create when you open the account). That first screen name is the one that America Online uses to track billing and account information, so it's yours for the long haul.

To delete a screen name, follow these steps:

1. Sign onto America Online with your master screen name and use the keyword **Names** to open the Create or Delete Screen Names dialog box. You can also open the Screen Names dialog box by clicking the My AOL button on the button bar and selecting Screen Names from the list that appears.

2. Double-click Delete a Screen Name in the item list and then click Continue in the dialog box that asks whether you really want to delete a screen name.

3. When Delete a Screen Name dialog box appears, click the doomed screen name to select it. Then click the Delete button to send that name into the Screen Name Netherworld.

All's not lost if you delete a screen name in error. Double-clicking the Restore a Screen Name item in the Create or Delete Screen Names dialog box leads you through the process of bringing that dead name back to life.

Switching Screen Names

Beginning with America Online version 4.0, members can change from one screen name to another with a click of the mouse (and a correct password). Switching your screen name comes in very handy for checking e-mail in a screen name that you use only for work before spending time relaxing on the system under your off-duty screen name. Another use is changing to a gaming screen name (which you use for live role-playing games) after cruising the system with your normal screen name.

To switch screen names, follow these steps:

1. Choose Sign Off⇨Switch Screen Name from the AOL menu bar.

2. Select the screen name you want switch to from the list of names in the Switch Screen Names dialog box that appears and click the Switch button. (A yellow envelope next to a screen name in this dialog box indicates that mail awaits you under that screen name.) A useful Switch Screen Name dialog box appears to tell you how long you spent online.

3. Click OK in the Switch Screen Name dialog box.

4. Enter your password into the Password dialog box that appears and click OK. The system churns for a moment, and then America Online bids you a hearty welcome under your new screen name.

Show Your Face with an Online Profile

Introduce yourself to the America Online community by creating a member profile (see Figure 3-4). Profiles enable you to share your interests as well as what drives you. Alert others to your sense of humor or sense of the sublime by including a personal quote at the end of your profile. Many times, members check profiles while interacting with others online — especially in chat rooms. A person's profile gives someone a picture of what you may be like. When you fill out your online profile form, you can include as little or as much information as you like.

Depending on how you use America Online, different screen names may require different member profiles. A home-business or work-related screen name, for example, may highlight your occupation, while a screen name devoted to perusing a hobby mentions that interest. Members who play online games create profiles that talk about their imaginary character's life and loves.

Create or change your online profile with keyword: **Profile**, which opens the Member Directory dialog box. Click the My Profile button to open your screen name's profile information and then fill in whatever information you want to share. Some members enter only their screen names, while others fill in every blank.

Figure 3-4:   Create a Member Profile to tell others about your interests.

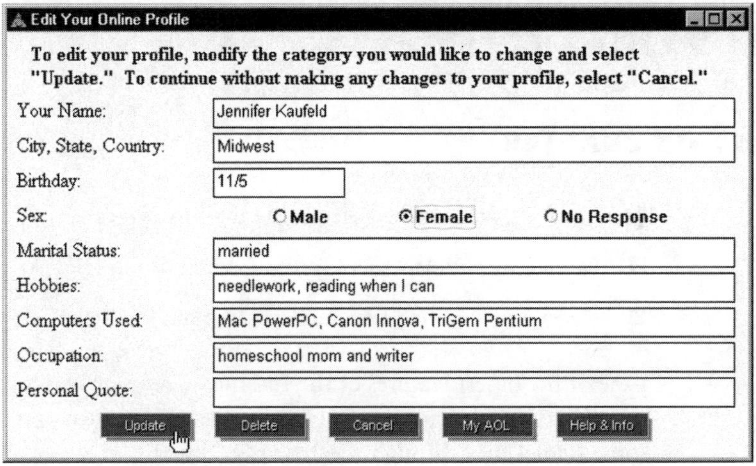

Edit Your Online Profile	

To edit your profile, modify the category you would like to change and select "Update." To continue without making any changes to your profile, select "Cancel."

Your Name:	Jennifer Kaufeld
City, State, Country:	Midwest
Birthday:	11/5
Sex:	○ Male ⊙ Female ○ No Response
Marital Status:	married
Hobbies:	needlework, reading when I can
Computers Used:	Mac PowerPC, Canon Innova, TriGem Pentium
Occupation:	homeschool mom and writer
Personal Quote:	

[Update] [Delete] [Cancel] [My AOL] [Help & Info]

Never include your address, phone number, or other personal information in a member profile. Remember that your profile is visible to anyone else using America Online. You may want to enter your region of the country or your state instead of city and state, if online privacy concerns you.

Don't believe everything that you read, especially in a member profile. Just as you have the freedom to create a pure fantasy profile, every other member has that right as well.

To find someone else's profile online, click the People button on the AOL button bar and select Get AOL Member Profile from the list that appears. Fill in the member's screen name, and click OK.

CHAPTER 4
USING E-MAIL

IN THIS CHAPTER

- Creating and sending electronic mail messages
- Managing the America Online Address Book
- Receiving attached files in electronic mail

One of the oldest features of the Internet, *electronic mail* (or *e-mail*) connects you to the digital world. Packed with opinions, e-mail flies through the Internet, filling e-mail boxes, sparking discussion, and providing a social outlet. With e-mail at your disposal, the weather outside doesn't matter — you can still connect with the people in your life (as long as they have an e-mail address).

With e-mail you can send messages requesting information about a company's products, keep in touch with family members close or far away, and establish new friendships with other AOL members you meet along your online journey. Share tips with classmates, alert a friend to a job opening, or pass that treasured recipe to the guests from your last party. This chapter focuses on the basic ins and outs of e-mail, such as sending messages, receiving e-mail, and keeping your computer safe from would-be e-mail hackers.

Sending Electronic Mail

To create your own e-mail messages and send your thoughts winging through cyberspace, just follow these steps:

1. Click the Write toolbar button. An e-mail window appears, ready for your missive (see Figure 4-1).

2. Enter the addressee's e-mail address in the Send To text box.

3. In the Subject text box, enter a few words that tell why you're writing.

4. Write your message in the large text box. If your message goes to an Internet recipient rather than to someone on AOL, you need to put your e-mail address under your signature. Some Internet services hide the information at the beginning of an e-mail message, and if the recipient doesn't already know your e-mail address, he can't reply to your message otherwise.

5. Click the Send Now button to send the e-mail message on its way.

Figure 4-1:   Send messages to friends far and near with AOL e-mail.

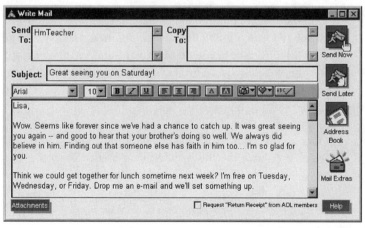

The buttons above the large text box in the Write Mail window let you spice up your message with color, different fonts, and formatting options. Experiment with them to make your messages stand out.

Sending unsolicited e-mail messages to groups of unsuspecting people is against America Online's Terms of Service. Whether you send a "new, cool business opportunity" message or a chain letter requesting people to forward it to their 500 closest friends, AOL has a name for it. They call e-mail like that *spam*, and the AOL Cops frown on it.

Much like the regular mail that you send via the U.S. Postal Service, once you send out a message you might not be able to get it back. Read through your e-mail *before* you send it to ensure that it says what you want it to say. Especially if emotions are high, killing a thoughtless e-mail message (by clicking the Close box in the upper right corner of the Write Mail window) is much easier than apologizing later for offending someone.

Reading Electronic Mail

If your AOL account contains mail, you hear a cheery "You've Got Mail" announcement when you sign on. The mailbox on the Welcome window also shows a yellow letter sticking out of it, and the words You Have Mail appear written underneath (see Figure 4-2).

To read your new mail, either click the Read button on the toolbar or click the full mailbox icon on the Welcome window. After your screen name's Online Mailbox window opens, double-click any message that looks interesting. The e-mail message opens, and you're on your way.

To reply to an e-mail message, just click the Reply button in the open e-mail message window to open the Write Mail window. The recipient's e-mail address is already filled in.

Figure 4-2:   You've got mail!

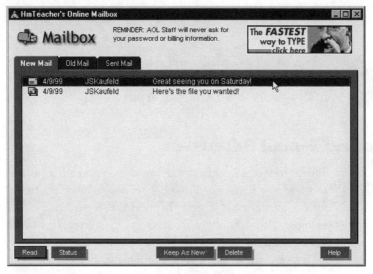

You may receive spam messages with blue underlined Internet links inviting you to visit this or that Web page. If you don't personally know the message sender, do *not* click the link. Such a link can lead you to a Web site that downloads a program into your computer that steals your AOL password or worse. Click the Delete button at the bottom of the e-mail message to erase it from your mailbox. If you don't know the e-mail sender, you're better off being cautious and keeping your computer safe.

Deleting Those Unwanted Messages

Plagued by junk e-mail messages? The ever-so-handy Delete button jumps to your rescue.

If you know you don't want to read a message in your online mailbox, you don't even need to open it. While perusing the list of new mail in your online mailbox, click the annoying message to highlight it and then click Delete at the bottom of the Online Mailbox window. Poof! It's history.

After you open an e-mail message, read it, and decide to give it a very short life, click the Delete button at the bottom of the open message to send it on its way.

After you kill an e-mail message by using the Delete button, it's out of your life forever. Nothing — not even the gurus at AOL — can ever bring it back to life.

Finding E-mail Addresses

What's your e-mail address and how do you find other people's addresses? To send e-mail to other people on America Online, the e-mail address is simply that person's screen name — for example, JSKaufeld (for yours truly). To receive e-mail from someone on the Internet, the Internet e-mail address that you want to give the sender is your screen name, all lowercase, with @aol.com at the end of it. Then your screen name becomes something like jskaufeld@aol.com.

To find someone else's e-mail address after they send you a message, click the Reply button to create a new e-mail message and then copy down the address that you see in the Send To text box of the mail window. If you want to send someone you know an e-mail message and you don't know the address, the best way to find out is to pick up the phone. Call them and ask — it's a whole lot faster than trying any other method.

Keeping an Online Address Book

For most AOL members, a huge chasm exists between sending frequent e-mail messages to someone and memorizing the person's e-mail address. Just because you use it all the time doesn't mean that you can recall the address over dinner at a restaurant.

America Online created the Address Book for members to store frequently used e-mail addresses. Opening the Address Book window is a whole lot easier than rifling through stacks of sticky notes to find that important person's e-mail address.

Keyword: **Address Book** opens the AOL Address Book (as shown in Figure 4-3). Click New Person to enter someone's name and e-mail address into the Address Book and then click OK. The window even includes a section for notes on how you met the person or why that person even exists in your Address Book. The Address Book stores this information last name first (if, of course, you included the last name when you created the entry). If you only use first names or nicknames in your Address Book, AOL alphabetized the entries with whatever you give it — look for Jill Smith under S, and your friend Bunny under B.

Figure 4-3:   Creating Address Book entries for friends and colleagues saves on desktop sticky-note clutter.

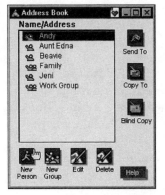

You can use your AOL Address Book for a number of purposes, as the following describes:

■   **Send e-mail to family members or friends a whole group at a time.** Just create one Address Book entry for the whole gang. To do so, click New Group in the Address Book window and then type in everyone's e-mail addresses — you can even mix AOL addresses with Internet Addresses in the same Group entry. The Address Book doesn't care one way or the other.

■ **Send e-mail to a person whose entry appears in the Address Book.** Click the Write button on the AOL toolbar to open the Write Mail window and then click the Address Book button to open your e-mail Address Book. Double-click any entry in the Address Book window, and that person's e-mail address appears in the Write Mail window's Send To text box. (If you click a Group entry, you see a bunch of e-mail addresses hop into the Write Mail window's Send To box, with each e-mail address separated by commas.)

■ **Add notes to the entry.** After you create a New Person or New Group Address Book entry, the New Person (Group) window contains a space for Notes — very handy if you keep e-mail addresses for people from all the parts of your life. Use the Notes section to jot down where you met the person, what projects you may be working on together, or any other pertinent information, such as hobbies you share.

Sooner or later, parting time comes to nearly all. When the day arrives and you need to delete your newfound friend from the Address Book, use the keyword **Address Book** to open the Address Book window and follow these steps:

1. Highlight the doomed entry in the Address Book window.

2. Click the Delete button. A panicked dialog box appears, asking you whether you're sure that you want to delete that item.

3. To send the entry into the nether reaches of cyberspace, click Yes. If you change your mind at the last minute, click No.

After you delete an Address Book entry, it's history. The only way to bring it back is to re-create it from scratch. Pause a second before you delete to make sure that you really want to be rid of the entry.

If your friend changes her Internet Service Provider, you can change her e-mail address without deleting it by clicking the Edit button in the Address Book window. Alter the address in the E-mail Address text box so that it matches your friend's new destination and click OK to save the changes.

Automatic AOL Brings Your Mail to You

America Online's *Automatic AOL* feature enables you to download incoming e-mail into your computer so that you can read it later offline. This feature comes in handy if your household uses only one phone line. Instead of spending an hour or two reading e-mail and tying up the phone line (which is very easy to do without realizing it), you can download the messages, read them as you have time, write replies, and then send those replies with the next Automatic AOL session you run.

Setting up Automatic AOL

Before using Automatic AOL for the first time, you need to tell the AOL software what you want it to do. Keyword: **Auto AOL** opens the Automatic AOL Walk-Through dialog box. The Automatic AOL Walk-Through dialog box gives you two options. If you want America Online to walk you through each step as you set up the Automatic AOL feature, follow these steps:

1. Click Continue at the bottom of the Automatic AOL Walk-Through dialog box. AOL then shows you a series of screens explaining each option.

2. Read each screen, answering the questions as you go. The software takes your answers and customizes Automatic AOL so that it does what you want.

One of the screens asks you to select the screen names that you want to use with Automatic AOL and then type in your password. If you feel uneasy about entering your password into the software, highlight any stars you see in the Password text boxes and press Back Space. This erases your password from this part of the software. Then click Continue.

Should you decide to leave your password in the screen, the software uses it *only* for Automatic AOL. You still need to type your password whenever you sign onto the system.

3. Continue answering each screen's question until you reach the Congratulations screen and then click OK in the Congratulations screen for the software to save the Automatic AOL settings.

Running Automatic AOL

After setting up Automatic AOL, using the feature to download e-mail is easy. If you run an Automatic AOL session this way, you begin the download session without relying on the Automatic AOL scheduler to do it for you. Just follow these steps:

1. First, sign onto America Online under the screen name you want to use with Automatic AOL (if you're not already on the system).

2. Click the Mail Center button on the toolbar and then choose Run Automatic AOL (FlashSessions) Now. The Run Automatic AOL Now dialog box hops to the screen (see Figure 4-4).

Figure 4-4:   Download your e-mail and sign off the system in one step by using Automatic AOL.

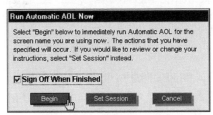

3. If you want the service to sign you off after running an Automatic AOL session, click the Sign Off When Finished check box to select it. Otherwise, leave the check box blank to resume your online wanderings after the Automatic AOL session finishes.

4. Click Begin to start the Automatic AOL download.

Attaching Files to E-mail Messages

The Attachments button at the bottom of the Write Mail window lets you send files along with e-mail messages. Use it to send documents such as last year's family newsletter or the proposal you drafted for your colleagues. You can also attach graphics such as a picture of the nieces and nephews or an electronic greeting card you create. After someone receives your e-mail and attachment, she can download the file into her computer (as the following section describes).

When you finish writing your e-mail, click the Attachments button to open the Attachments dialog box (see Figure 4-5). Click the Attach button and browse through your hard drive to find the file you want to send. Double-clicking the file name in the Attach window that appears drops it into the Attachments dialog box. You see it appear in the Attachments dialog box.

Repeat to attach another file or click OK to return to the e-mail message you were working on. The file name(s) you selected appear next to the attachments button in the Write Mail window. Then send the message as usual. America Online compacts the files (if you attach more than one) and sends them along with the e-mail message to the recipient.

Figure 4-5: Attach files from your hard drive and send them to friends via e-mail.

Downloading Files from E-mail Messages

When Aunt Sally sends you a photo from last year's family reunion, download it into your computer for a good look. Anyone can attach text files, programs, graphics, and sound files to e-mail messages. In fact, by using America Online's attachment feature (described in the preceding section), another AOL member can send you several files in one message.

You know a particular e-mail message has an attached file by the small blue disk that you see peeking out from under the letter icon in your Online Mailbox window. To download the file, open the e-mail message and click Download Now (see Figure 4-6).

Figure 4-6:   Download attached files from friends and colleagues.

> Here's the file you wanted!
>
> Subj: **Here's the file you wanted!**
> Date: 4/9/99 12:43:02 PM US Eastern Standard Time
> From: JSKaufeld
> To: HmTeacher
>
> File: TTNIC10.TXT (433882 bytes)
> DL Time (26400 bps): < 5 minutes
>
> Hi!
>
> I found the file you were looking for. This Titanic document talks about several
> reasons why the ship sank. I hope it helps.
>
> Enjoy!
>
> Jenny
>
> Reply   Forward   Reply All   Add Address
>
> Download Now   Download Later   Delete   Prev   2 of 2   Help

Never, ever download an attached file from someone you don't know well. The file may contain a program designed to steal your password or wreck your computer. The e-mail messages themselves are safe — the attached files are what can cause damage.

Eluding Viruses

Computer *viruses* create big news these days. Designed by programmers seeking to damage someone's equipment (or at the very least to pull a practical joke), these programs do everything from stealing your AOL password to destroying every program on your hard drive.

A true computer virus acts like poison ivy. It starts as a little program somewhere in your system and then replicates itself all through your computer's hard drive, much as poison ivy sprouts in one little place and, before you know it, appears all over your arm. Most of the time, a virus acts slowly, so it may take a while before it does anything bizarre to your system. A virus, over time, takes up lots of space on your hard drive and often destroys files a little bit at a time.

A *Trojan Horse program*, often called a virus, doesn't usually reproduce itself. Instead, it's designed to install itself on your computer's hard drive and destroy programs (often the programs at the lowest level that make your computer work).

Here are some things to keep in mind about viruses while exploring on AOL:

■ A text-only e-mail message can't include a virus. Text files do *not* carry viruses, and e-mail is text. Any downloadable files attached to the message, however, are another matter — including document files.

■ Be aware that the "Warning: Such and Such is a virus e-mail" messages going around and around on the Internet are usually hoaxes. These messages are designed to scare people and clog the Internet airways with useless e-mail messages. *Viruses don't exist in e-mail text.*

■ Clicking underlined Internet link text inside an e-mail message *can* lead you to a Web site designed to install a Trojan Horse on your system. Never visit a link you receive in an e-mail message unless you know the person sending you the e-mail.

■ You can visit AOL's Virus Information Center (keyword: **Virus**) for computer virus facts and news about popular virus hoaxes.

CHAPTER 5

FINDING YOUR WAY AROUND

IN THIS CHAPTER

- Using keywords to navigate through AOL
- Remembering the best areas with Favorite Places
- Jumping from here to there with hyperlinks

Part of the fun of America Online is mousing around — clicking this button or that hyperlink until you find yourself delightfully far from where you began, possessing more knowledge about Endangered Seed Sprouting than you ever dreamed possible. Hours may pass as you travel up one alley and down another, exploring online areas you never imagined.

America Online contains a wealth of information on nearly every subject imaginable. Add to that the contents of the Web, and you can literally explore for years and never see it all. Consider the possibility of always making a new discovery part of the fun of online life. No matter what you've seen before, each year (or month or day) brings new articles to read and new online areas to experience. This chapter includes the basics of getting around online. Whether you fall in love with keywords or you just want to see where you've been, this chapter helps you arrive at your goal with the least amount of frustration.

Keywords Open Online Areas

Think of the America Online keyword as a secret password. No matter where you are online, you can open a Keyword dialog box and type the password .Before you can say, "Shazam," the software churns and a new window opens on-screen, ripe for exploration.

Almost every window (and certainly each main area) online has its own keyword. As you click through the system, look down in the lower-right corner of the window. Look for a notation that reads Keyword: or KW: with one or more words following it. These words are what you enter into the Keyword dialog box so that it works its magic.

Open the Keyword dialog box by clicking the Keyword button on the browser bar. Then type the keyword into the text field (see Figure 5-1) and click Go — and you're off!

Figure 5-1:   Enter a keyword to open an online area.

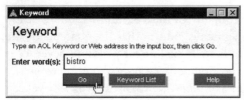

Bored? Try typing miscellaneous words into the Keyword dialog box, such as names of cities around the world. Even if you get a Keyword Not Found message in return, you still find new possibilities to explore by reading the list of alternate keywords in the Keywords Found dialog box that appears.

For a huge list of keywords (some current, many not) use keyword: **Keyword**.

Navigating an AOL Window

At first glance, you notice that virtually any AOL area resonates with color, underlined text, and inviting buttons. Although each looks a little different in design, all America Online areas share certain features, as the following list describes:

■ **Hyperlinks:** Clicking any underlined text gives you the same results as clicking a button: Doing so opens a window or text document so that you can read and explore.

■ **Banner Ads:** Most windows feature a banner ad — it's the large rectangle in the upper or lower corner of the window that opens a corporate advertisement window after you click it. Companies pay to put these ads on America Online, just as they pay to place an advertisement in the newspaper or a magazine. Don't feel compelled to click any of them, however, unless you want to know what the company offers.

■ **Buttons:** Each window contains *buttons* of some sort that lead you on to other windows containing more or different information. To open a new window, click its button.

■ **Message and Chat buttons:** Each area also uses features such as online chat rooms and message boards to create a community for members with an interest in that subject. Because people who work at home may or may not find interests in common with Beanie Baby collectors or Extreme Sports fanatics, each area creates (and prides itself on) its own collection of scheduled chats, open chat rooms, and message boards. In these rooms and windows, members discuss topics near and dear to their hearts. Look for buttons or text entries that read *Chat, Discussions, Messages, Boards,* or some derivation.

■ **Featured Areas:** Channel windows contain a *Featuring* area in the lower-left corner. Look there for large areas that relate somehow to the window you're in. Instead of opening only one window, clicking these Featuring buttons reveals an entire new topical area to explore. The difference between what you see after clicking these buttons and regular buttons is like the difference between turning to a page in a book and turning to a chapter — you get to both the same way, but one holds more stuff than the other.

■ **Featured articles within areas:** Large areas, although they don't use the Featuring approach, still use large graphic buttons to entice you to their coolest contents. Clicking any prominent button in an online window takes you to a featured article or featured subarea for that area.

■ **Departments:** Most areas and channels place their *department buttons* somewhere near the middle of the window. Ranging anywhere in number from four to as many as ten, these departments divide the area into sizeable chunks. Want to see what vendors list items for sale? Look for a Shopping or Shop at (*Area Name*) button.

No matter which window you find yourself in, check out the Fun 'n' Games or Humor department if the area lists one. There you find trivia, polls, and other amusements designed around the area's topic.

Depending on the amount of traffic an area gets and the time its managers can afford on area maintenance, some of the older windows you find may look quite different than the majority you see online (see Figure 5-2). These areas generally contain bold text explaining its contents; hover the mouse over any portion of the text and click after the pointer turns into a hand.

Also look for the area's contents in an item list box. The following steps tell how to locate content in the older windows:

1. If the list fills the little item box, click the scroll bar at the right side to see the remainder of the list.

2. Scroll up and down, reading the items in the list.

3. Double-click any item that appeals to you to open that subarea's window.

Figure 5-2: Read the document, click the button, and explore an area.

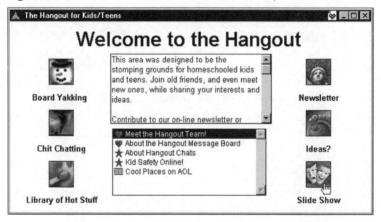

Older areas also sport large, square icons with text underneath explaining where each icon leads. Treat them the same as buttons and click away.

Favorite Places

If you visit an online area that you want to see again, mark it as a Favorite Place. Nearly every window on America Online or the Web appears with an icon at the upper-right corner of the window. This icon looks like a red heart on a white sheet of paper. That's your *Favorite Place* button. With that little icon in the corner, the online world is yours for the collecting.

To mark a window as a Favorite Place, just click the heart icon. A small dialog box appears, asking whether you want to add the window to your list of favorites, among other things. Click the Add to Favorites button, and America Online bookmarks that Web site or online area as a Favorite Place.

To use a Favorite Place after you mark it, click the Favorite Places toolbar button. The bottom of the pull-down menu lists all your Favorite Places. Click one, and that site or area opens on-screen.

Hyperlinks

Underlined words in blue decorate nearly every screen on America Online and the Web. Known as *hyperlinks* — and often simply called just *links* — these words function as a bridge from one window to another. When you click the underlined text, it opens another area or window on-screen.

Hyperlinks give online denizens quick ways to jump from one related topic to another. You can also use them to explore more about a topic. Sometimes a page designer writes a little bit of information and then adds the word <u>More</u> as a hyperlink. If the introduction merely whets your appetite, click the link to discover more. On the other hand, if that first paragraph or two tells you more than you ever want to know, skip the link and continue browsing. By skipping the link, you don't waste time watching something load on-screen that you find less than enthusing.

Figure 5-3:   Click a link that looks interesting to access additional information.

> Baseball Chat: Join us each day
> as we discuss the games, the
> players and all the day's news.
>
> ⬤ Hockey Publications: Get the inside
> scoop from those in the know.
>
> ⬤ Golf Chat: Talk about the Masters
> and those on top of the leaderboard.

To find out where a hyperlink goes while browsing through America Online, pass the mouse pointer over the underlined text without clicking. An information box pops up, giving you the Web address connected to the hyperlink. If the link takes you to an area that's part of AOL, the box says `On AOL Only`.

Hyperlinks make keeping track of where you've been downright easy. When you return to a window displaying a hyperlink that you already explored, the words appear in a different color, generally pink or purple. This color change saves you a world of time as you search for a topic on the Web. Each time you return to that list of 4,000 possible sites about vegetarianism, the ones you've already seen show up in the alternate color.

Beware clicking a hyperlink that some random person sends you in an e-mail. If you don't know the person writing to you, *don't* follow the link. It could lead directly to a program designed to steal your password or destroy part of your hard drive. Be safe — follow links only from friends and explore on your own if you want to find something instead of following a suspicious e-mail message link.

Getting Back Where You Were

You just spent two hours exploring AOL, and you want to visit that third window you opened . . . the one about pets. But you don't remember the keyword. (Psst . . . it's keyword:

Pets.) Before you decide to try it again another day, go up to the browser bar and click the down arrow next to the text box. A drop-down list appears, showing you the places you visited recently online (see Figure 5-4). Unless you opened so many windows that your first ones scroll off the bottom of the list, you should find that Pets window somewhere near the bottom of the list.

As you look at the list, you see some entries that appear as, for example, `AOL: Grandstand`. These entries take you to areas within America Online itself. Listings that appear as `http://www.tobinlab.com` or `Vintage Knitting`, on the other hand, open the Web browser and load a Web site.

Figure 5-4:   Visit an earlier area with a little help from the browser bar.

Looking at Topics Channel by Channel

Most AOL members begin exploring the system looking for a particular topic. Whether a sports area, financial information, or the idea of shopping online is what thrills you, America Online organizes it all underneath the 19 buttons in the Channels window.

Use the Channels menu to browse and discover online areas that really interest you. Because of the design of America Online, you can click forever and still feel as though you're getting no closer to your goal. In an attempt to alleviate that feeling, Table 5-1 gives you an idea of what channel to try, depending on exactly what you want to find. (For some *really* neat online areas that sometimes get buried in the channels, take a look at Chapter 10.)

Table 5-1: AOL Channel Finder

If You Want to Find	Try This Channel
AOL's Canadian service	International channel
Auto racing	Sports channel
Auto repair	Interests channel
Autos (buying/selling)	Local channel
Aviation	Interests channel
Baby-name suggestions	Families channel
Books/Reading	Entertainment channel, Influence channel, Interests channel
Business News	News channel
Buying online	Shopping channel
Celebrity info	Influence channel, Entertainment channel
Cheerleading	Sports channel
Collectible Cards	Sports channel, Games channel, Games Insider department
Collectibles	Interests channel
Current events and stories	AOL Today channel
Dining out	Local channel
Ethnic Diversity	Lifestyles channel, International channel
Finding a job or creating a resume	WorkPlace channel
Free online role-playing games	Games channel, Games Insider department

Continued

Table 5-1:   AOL Channel Finder *(Continued)*

If You Want to Find	Try This Channel
Genealogy channel	Families channel, Interests
Gourmet food, wine, and cigars	Influence channel
Historical Reinactment	Interests channel
Horoscopes	News channel, Life department
Hotel Reservations	Travel channel
Hunting	Sports channel
Illnesses	Health channel
Kids online	Kids Only channel
MTV Online	Entertainment channel
Music releases (classical, alternative, rock, or country)	Entertainment channel
Online courses (almost free)	Research & Learn channel
Online courses (free)	Computing channel
Pen pals	International channel, Local channel
Puzzles	Games channel
Raising kids	Families channel
Recipes and menu planning help	Interests channel
Real estate & home buying	Personal Finance channel
Religion	Lifestyles channel
Romance and Weddings	Lifestyles channel
Science Fair project ideas	Research & Learn channel
Self Improvement	Lifestyles channel
Seniors	Lifestyles channel
Software downloads (free)	Computing channel
Sports	Sports channel, Local channel, International channel

If You Want to Find	*Try This Channel*
Support groups	Health channel
Starting a business	WorkPlace channel
Tax information	Personal Finance channel
Thesaurus	Research & Learn channel
Tightwads (frugal living)	Interests channel
Trivia	Games channel, WorkPlace channel's WorkPlace Humor department, Lifestyles Channel's Spirituality department
TV listings	Entertainment channel
Vacation ideas	Travel channel
Weather	News channel
Web page information	Computing channel
Women's Issues	Lifestyles channel

CHAPTER 6

LOCATING THINGS ONLINE

IN THIS CHAPTER

- Finding cool stuff available on AOL

- Getting free (or at least cheap) programs

- Searching the Internet for unusual topics

The online world overflows with cool stuff. Whether you want files for your computer, gardening hints, or the latest UFO propaganda, stuff abounds in cyberspace. Unfortunately, this wealth of information is yours to read or download only if you know where to find it. And finding stuff online can sometimes prove tricky.

This chapter gives you tips for using AOL to locate information online. From the halls of AOL itself all the way to the universe of the Web, cool areas await you. Visit a few and broaden your online horizons.

Finding Stuff on AOL

Locating things on America Online may prove the easiest thing you've done since you munched that last candy bar. On the other hand, the process may give the term *frustration* new meaning. The America Online search engine, *AOL Search*, helps you locate those elusive areas, as do as the channels' *Search & Explore* departments. Sometimes.

Using AOL Search

The keyword **AOL Search** opens the AOL Search dialog box. Or you can just click Search in the Channels window. Either way, you end up with a window that looks much like the one shown in Figure 6-1.

Figure 6-1:   Looking for something online? Try AOL Search first.

Enter the topic into the text box and click the Search button. AOL chugs and churns and then proudly produces a window displaying a list of its findings. Double-click one of the entries to visit a listed area. If the system returns fewer selections than you like, try a different but similar search term. Entering **vehicle**, for example, returns only 10 possible areas, while typing **car** gives you 37 results and **auto** offers 60. Of course, the results of **auto** include areas that cover *auto*matic banking as well as the auto with four wheels. Just because the search engine gives you loads of stuff doesn't mean that the results are what you need.

Using Search & Explore

Each of AOL's channels includes a Search & Explore department. Generally placed as the last button in the department list, most people don't notice the Search & Explore buttons much. If you know that you want an area that *should* fit under a particular channel, however, the Search & Explore department may contain exactly what you need.

When you open any channel's Search & Explore department, a window greets you with a list of that channel's content areas in alphabetical order. For some searches, a trip through this list locates the information you seek.

If browsing the contents list still leaves you high and dry, try using that channel's individual search engine. It combs the contents of its particular channel to find more specific things for you. To use a channel's search engine, follow these steps:

1. Click the Search button in the channel's Search & Explore window. A small Search dialog box appears in the upper-left corner of the screen.

2. Enter the search term into the Enter search word(s) text box of this dialog box.

3. Unless you want articles no more than a week old, click the downward-pointing arrow next to the Find articles within the last drop-down list box and then select a more reasonable period of time from the list that appears — such as month or year.

4. Tell AOL how long you're willing to wait for results by selecting a time in the Maximum time you want to wait drop-down list box. The default setting is one minute; if you want to wait longer for results, you can select two minutes or five minutes from the drop-down list.

5. Click the Start Searching button to send the request on its way.

6. When AOL returns a list of possible matches for your search, click any of the underlined links to read the document.

Looking for Snazzy Software

How much software can one hard drive hold? Test your theories with the downloadable software available on America Online and the Internet.

Browse through the keyword **Download Center** to find programs that play games, help with finances, assist with algebra or chemistry terms, or do practically anything else you may need. AOL organizes software files by category and subcategory, so to find a spreadsheet helper for work, for example, you begin with the Business and Finance folder.

If you know exactly what you want but you don't know where to look for it, use click the Software Search button in the Download Center window to access the Software Search system. Click the Shareware button in the Filesearch dialog box that appears, and the Software Search window comes to life (see Figure 6-2). Tell America Online what you need, and it checks its massive storage areas to see whether it has a copy to offer you.

Figure 6-2:   Comb AOL's archives for that elusive file.

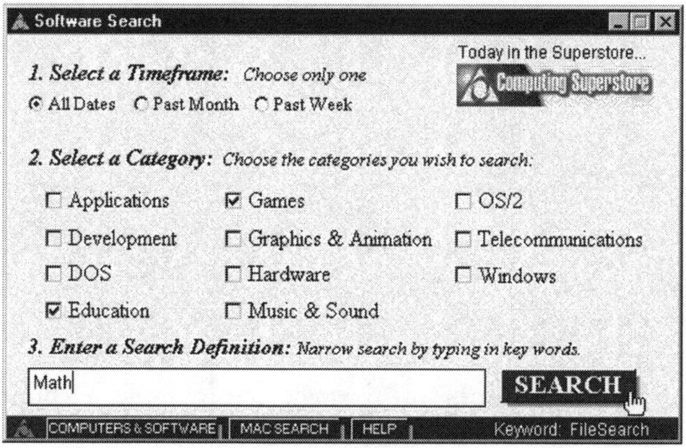

To download software from the Internet, start with www.download.com, a software site operated by C|Net, the Computer Network television people. Although C|Net may not keep a billion files on hand for downloading, they certainly offer enough to keep a software searcher busy.

If you download any files from the Internet, test them with virus-detecting software *before* you install them on your computer and try to play or use them. (All files in America Online's archives are virus-free. A staff member checks each file before releasing it to the software libraries.)

Shareware means that it's free to download, but if you like it, you need to pay for it. Shareware programs come with contact information so that you can send the programmer what he requests — sometimes he collects post cards and wants a post card from your part of the world. Other programmers request anywhere from $5 to $30 for keeping and using their software.

Searching the Web

Turn to the Web on those days when you want the truly esoteric. Looking for information on lacemakers worldwide? Definitely a topic for Web searches. Need the gene mapping for a specific chromosome? A Web search probably turns up more useful information than you can find browsing through America Online alone.

Open a Web search engine by typing the site's address into the browser bar and then clicking Go. The Web browser opens, loads the search engine, and awaits your next instructions.

Internet search engines sort through sites by topic. To hunt for sites on the Web, enter the topic into the search text box and then click a Search or Go button. The search engine works through its database and then presents a list of sites that match your search term (or so the search engine thinks). You then must read through each site's description and decide whether it's what you're looking for.

Tip

Search engines rank their results according to how closely they matched your original term. So look near the top of the list for the most relevant sites to your question. If the search engine returns more than a reasonable number of sites — and especially if the sites number in the thousands or tens of thousands — you may consider re-searching with a more narrow search topic. Typing **Mercury Comet** as your search topic, for example, returns a much more dedicated Web site list than simply entering **cars** in the Search text box.

Several different Web search engines exist on the Internet; each one contains various strengths and weaknesses. Below you'll find descriptions of three of the most popular search engines (including one owned by America Online). To see how these search systems compare with one another, you may want to search for the same term in all three and then look to see if the results differ.

AOL NetFind

America Online's own Internet search system, the *AOL NetFind* site also contains *Time Savers* — preselected searches on popular topics such as job or apartment hunting. Each link leads to several sites that AOL has already screened for usefulness so that you don't need to.

You can also use NetFind as a regular search engine by typing the topic into the text box near the top of the NetFind page and then clicking Search (see Figure 6-3). NetFind returns a list of Editor's Picks Web sites, which may or may not match your exact intent; look below the Editor's Picks for individual Web sites that the search engine gathers. Find one that you like and click the site's hyperlink to explore.

Figure 6-3: Use AOL NetFind to ferret out interesting sites.

Open AOL NetFind by typing its Web address into the browser bar text box (www.aol.com/netfind) or by clicking the Internet toolbar button and then selecting AOL NetFind from the list that appears.

AltaVista

The *AltaVista* search engine (at www.altavista.com) allows you to ask a question in real English . . . or any other language from Dutch to Latvian. Rather than distilling the question to its essential word or words, you can actually ask AltaVista a full-fledged question — such as "Where can I find economic information for France?"

If the questions befuddles AltaVista, the search engine gives you several Web sites which may or may not be close to what you want. If your search results show little or nothing you actually need, look near the top of the results page for questions that AltaVista suggests to help refine the search. Select one of these, if it applies, and the engine happily goes forth to find sites for you.

Yahoo!

One of the most celebrated Web search engines — and a personal favorite (probably because its site address is so easy to remember) — is *Yahoo!* (at www.yahoo.com). After the site loads, you can click a hyperlink from its list of 14 major topics to begin a huge Web-site browsing mission, or you can try to narrow the search by entering a word or two that describes the subject you need.

Tip

If you attempt a Web search on any search engine and it returns absolutely nothing, check to make sure that you spelled the words correctly and put them in the correct grammatical form, especially if you're using Yahoo!. Adding an *-ing* ending to the end of a word, for example, may seem a piddling error, but to the Web site frantically searching for *living* instead of *live,* the difference appears massive.

CHAPTER 7

CHATTING AND USING INSTANT MESSAGES

IN THIS CHAPTER

- Chatting with other members
- Locating scheduled chats online
- Finding a chat room
- Sending and receiving instant messages

Conversation makes the world go 'round, and America Online is no different. From huge online auditoriums to one-on-one interactive messages, AOL's virtual halls resound with chatter. Members meet to discuss hobbies, join online support groups, listen to scheduled speakers, or relax. Warm up your fingers and join the party.

Organized Online Chats

Nearly every hour of the day, some area of AOL schedules an organized chat. Whether a huge event drawing hundreds of people or a small, intimate gathering of ten likeminded souls, chats that begin at a certain time and date allow members to gather and talk about those issues dearest to their hearts.

AOL Live

For the biggest events of the season (or at least the upcoming couple of days) visit AOL Live (keyword **AOL Live**) and peek at the upcoming guest schedule (see Figure 7-1). Authors, sports figures, and newsmakers regularly appear (as well as an occasional celebrity) to discuss upcoming releases, current events, or the world as they see it.

Figure 7-1:   Look for a scheduled event in AOL Live.

AOL Live contains a complete listing of the "big" events —
those events that appeal to a wide range of members. The item
box lists events for today and tomorrow. To see events for the
next several days, click the Coming Attractions button.

When the event's about to start, click on the event's link in
the event list. When the window describing the event opens,
look for a Go to the Event button. Clicking that button takes
you to one of America Online's large auditoriums, which
looks like a chat room on steroids (see Figure 7-2). A small
box at the right side of the window lists the people on stage,
usually an online host and a special guest.

If you type a sentence into the chat room text box at the bottom of the screen, that text does *not* go to the speaker.
Instead, it appears in the large chat window with a number
next to it — for example, (13). This number means that
you're speaking to other members in your row, which this
time is row 13.

To ask a question or send a comment to the guest speaker,
click the Participate in event button at the right side of the

window, as shown in Figure 7-2. Enter your comment or question into the dialog box that appears, and click next to Ask a question or Send a Comment.

Figure 7-2: An AOL auditorium.

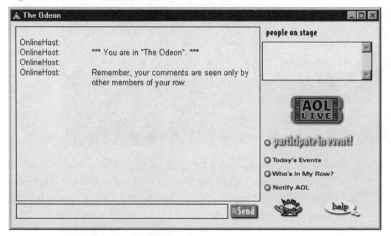

Online areas

Each channel (and even individual online areas) schedules online chats where members gather to hear a scheduled guest speaker. Usually, an online area's guest speaker is an AOL member who frequents the area and has an expertise in something that may interest other members, so the chat host asks him to share for an hour or so.

Many scheduled chats simply reserve a room so that anyone interested in that topic can hang out and chatter. Especially in areas such as homeschooling, parenting, some work-related areas, and seniors, scheduled chats tend to be times to hang out with friends and relax. The area schedules the chat to ensure that the room is free, but the topic itself is open as long as it loosely matches the online area.

Hanging Out in the Chat Rooms

Discuss, debate, and congregate in various online chat rooms. Whether an online area sponsors particular chat rooms or members create them, look in the chat rooms for lively chatter. With no schedule to keep, general chat room conversation ebbs and flows as members float in and out. While these chat rooms sometimes stick to the topic at hand (the room's name or online area dictates its overall topic), often the chatter wanders from laundry to sports and back again.

■ Wander into one of the international chat rooms and broaden your horizons by talking to members halfway around the world.

■ When you find a chat room you really like, mark it as a Favorite Place so you can find it again easily.

■ Keep in mind the Golden Rule in the rooms: Chat with others like you'd want them to chat with you.

■ One evening, visit a chat room you'd never pick on your own, like a room dedicated to business, sports, education, or news. Read the text as it scrolls by, and learn about something new.

Area rooms

Each online area devotes space to at least one chat room. Generally, if the area offers two chat rooms, it reserves one for scheduled chats while leaving the other for spontaneous conversation. Available 24 hours a day, these open chat rooms become places to meet friends and share ideas.

To find an online area's chat room, visit the area of your choice and look for a button marked Chat or Chat/Messages. There you see buttons or icons for chat rooms and a posted schedule if one of the rooms is hosting only scheduled chats. If you see no posted schedule, the room is open to all.

People Connection rooms

AOL's People Connection overflows with chat room options. Whether you want to discuss the arts in a foreign language or talk about the latest current events, the People Connection chat rooms provide areas to discuss virtually any topic under the sun.

AOL staff members create these particular chat rooms. To find a chat in the People Connection chat rooms, follow these steps:

1. Use keyword **People Connection** to open the People Connection window. Chapter 5 gives you the scoop on using keywords.

2. Click the Find a Chat button. The Find a Chat window opens.

3. Click to highlight a category (Life, Friends, and so on) in the Created by People Connection item list. The list box contents on the right change to show the selected category's available rooms (see Figure 7-3).

Figure 7-3: Search for a chat that meets your interests or your mood.

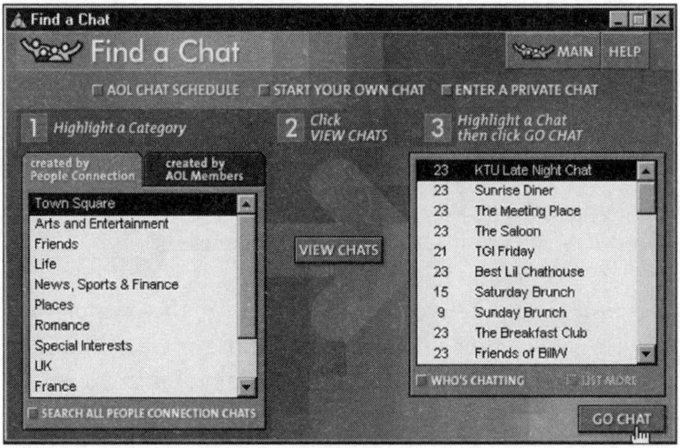

4. Double-click the name of a chat room that interests you in the list of available rooms. If the room isn't full, the room's window opens on-screen.

If the room already has 24 people chatting, then AOL displays a message informing you that That room's full and asks whether you want to visit another room just like the one you chose. Generally, the overflow room has exactly the same name as the original except that it attaches a number to the end of the name. Auto Addicts, for example, becomes Auto Addicts2 in an overflow chat room.

5. To join the conversation after the chat room window opens, enter your thoughts into the text field at the bottom of the screen and click Send. The text appears in the large text window, where everyone can see it.

Member rooms

America Online gives members the capability to create chat rooms that anyone can visit. If you find your interests tending toward the esoteric and think of a topic lacking in the People Connection rooms, browse the member chats.

To locate a member chat, follow these steps:

1. Use keyword **People Connection** to open the People Connection window.

2. Click Find a Chat to open the Find a Chat window and see the chat-room list.

3. Click the Created by AOL members tab at the top of the left hand item list. The screen flickers for a moment and then seems to return with the same categories. Actually, the categories list remains the same, but if you glance at the item list at the right side of the window, you see all the room names change.

4. Highlight a category and then browse for a chat room in the items list on the right.

5. Double-click the name of any room that looks interesting in the chat-room list to open that room.

Private rooms

For those days when you want to talk to only a few close friends, America Online lets members create private chat rooms. To enter someone else's private chat room, you need to know the name of the room. If you want people to visit your private chat, you need to give them the room's name, because they won't be able to find out any other way. Unlike the other online chat rooms, private rooms are exactly that. Private. No other members can access your private chat unless they think up the same name you did.

To create or visit a private chat room, use keyword **Private Chat** to open the Private Chat dialog box shown in Figure 7-4. Enter the name of your room in the text field and click Go Chat to transport yourself there.

Figure 7-4:   Think of a good name for your chat room.

The same Private Chat dialog box works whether you want to create a private room or visit one someone else created. If you request a room not currently open, AOL creates it for you.

Try to think of creative names for your chat rooms. "Hello" may be easy for friends to remember, but the Hello private chat room generally contains about 15 people who all had the same idea.

Periodically, someone may drop into your private chat unin- vited. The person just happens to hit on the same chat room name you did. Give the person a second. Generally other members leave without comment or with a "Sorry." If the intruder looks like she's thinking of hanging around, gently suggest that this is a private chat and that perhaps she could think of a different room name.

Instant Messages

If you spend any time online at all, sooner or later, a little chat window appears in the upper left corner of your screen displaying a typed message such as "Hello?" Known as an *Instant Message* (or *IM*), these little online notes allow mem- bers to chat one on one.

Instant Messages are handy if you're in a chat room and want to discuss something off topic with another chat room attendee. They're also useful when you want to connect with a friend currently online, but neither of you happens to be in the same chat room (or any chat room at all, for that matter).

Instant messenger

Internet users can also install a program called Instant Mes- senger (which America Online provides) to chat with AOL members via IMs. If you receive an Instant Message from an Internet Instant Messenger user, a small dialog box appears asking whether you want to receive the message. Click OK and the normal Instant Message window appears on-screen. Keyword: **Instant Messenger** tells you how sign up your friends who use an Internet Service Provider so they can chat with you via AOL.

Receiving Instant Messages

To receive an Instant Message that appears on-screen, click the Respond button. The window becomes larger, revealing a second, lower text box. Type your reply into the lower text box and click Send. Your reply then appears in the upper text box, under the sender's comment.

Periodically, you may receive an Instant Message requesting password or credit card information or sending lewd comments. Both these activities are against AOL's Terms of Service. Report the sender by clicking the Notify AOL button at the bottom of the Instant Message window.

Sending Instant Messages

Use Instant Messages to chat with friends while you read e-mail or share tips about great online areas. Whether you send an Instant Message to catch up with a friend or share knowledge, these handy little interactive notes help keep you in touch with members online.

Keyword **IM** opens the Instant Message window (see Figure 7-5). Enter the screen name of the person you want to chat with, type in a message, and click Send. The window appears in the upper-left corner of the other member's screen, and you're ready to chat the hours away.

Figure 7-5: Send an Instant Message to an online friend.

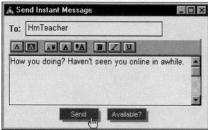
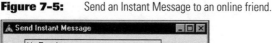

CHAPTER 8
JOINING AN ONLINE DISCUSSION

IN THIS CHAPTER

- Reading an online area's message boards
- Finding Internet newsgroups
- Reading and replying to newsgroup messages

Late at night or before the sun rises in the morning, your online buddies might be snoozing instead of spending time with you in a chat room or Instant Message. Take advantage of those quiet times to explore a favorite online area's *message board,* where members post and respond to each other's questions and comments.

Although e-mail is as private as you want it to be and chat rooms require both bodies present at their computers, message boards (also known as *discussion boards*) excel at carrying conversations from member to member, sometimes for weeks or months at a time.

So sharpen your digital pencil, find an online area you like, and join the community. For the most part, the members who leave messages on the boards are the same members you meet in the area's chat rooms. Message boards offer yet another way to build an online community.

Using Message Boards

Think of a *message board* as a cooperative letter, in which each member of an entire group of people contribute a paragraph or two (or perhaps only a sentence at a time). Read as an entire missive, the letter tells a story from several points of view. Because the message boards are public, any AOL member can read and comment on their contents. People being people, however, not many members range through various message boards to leave random notes. Most of the time, members find a message board because the topic interests them, and they visit that board's messages over and over again for months — or even years.

Message boards are the perfect format if you fall into one of the following categories:

■ You want to know other members' ideas about a certain topic.

■ You need an answer to a question, but you don't need it immediately.

■ You want to meet members with interests in the same subjects that interest you.

To open a message board, follow these steps:

1. Visit any AOL area. (For instructions on how to visit an AOL area, see Chapter 5.)

2. Click the button for messages. The exact name of the button differs depending on the area, but the idea is usually clear. Look for a Messages button, a Boards button, a Discussion Boards button, or a Chat/Messages button. After you click the button, a message-board window opens on-screen. Several entries in the window's item list box beckon for your attention.

3. Double-click any entry that looks interesting to open that message board or folder. Figure 8-1, shows the Hot Topics Message Board.

Figure 8-1:   Select a topic from the message board list for an evening's reading.

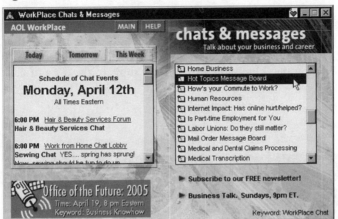

Remember from your earliest days the stacking ring baby toy with the six plastic doughnuts that fit on the plastic-rod base? First came the red ring and under that another and then another until you reached the purple (or was it orange?) ring at the very bottom of the stack. America Online's message boards can be like that toy. If the first folder you open reveals only more folders, keep clicking. Sooner or later, you reach the sticky-note-with-pin message board level. That's where the messages live.

Reading Message-Board Messages

Reading the messages that others post in a message board tells you what the other members think and gives you a good idea about which topics may or may not be appropriate for the board. To read a message on the message boards, follow these steps:

1. Click the message board button in any online area. The message board's window opens.

2. Double-click one of the message-board entries in the item list that appears. The icon in front of the message board looks like a sticky note with a pin sticking in it.

3. A list of current messages appears for that message-board topic. Highlight any message topic in the list and click the List All button to open it, as shown in Figure 8-2. A message window opens.

Figure 8-2: Need a thought for the day? Check the message boards.

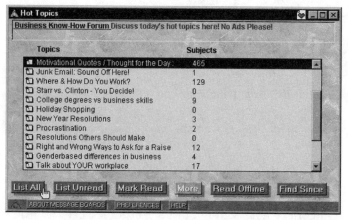

4. To move to the next message in the list, click the Subject button. If anyone replied to the open message, the Next Post button will be active. Click Next Post to read responses to the message currently on-screen.

The arrows on the Subject and Next Post buttons tell you which direction you're moving — up or down the message list.

After you read the messages under a particular board once and you return to the main message-board window, you can highlight the message topic again and click the List Unread button at the bottom of the window. Only the new messages you haven't seen yet now appear on the list. Clicking this button saves you time you'd otherwise spend scrolling through old messages that you've already read.

Posting to the Boards

Although no one minds if you lurk on your favorite message boards (reading all the messages without throwing in your two cents' worth or asking any questions), becoming part of the community is hard if you remain faceless. The two-way communication and multiple postings are what keep the message boards humming. Like any conversation between friends, the postings ebb and flow; sometimes you find a ton of new messages as you check your favorite boards. Other times, nary a soul seems to have visited.

Join the discussion by posting a reply or starting a new conversation within a message board. Just follow these steps:

1. Find a message that begs for your opinion and click Reply.

2. The Reply window opens with the subject line and the name of the person to whom you're replying already entered.

3. To include some of the original text in your reply, highlight text in the Original Message Text box and click the Quote button, as shown in Figure 8-3. The quoted text jumps to the Reply Window text box, complete with a quotation mark.

4. Type your response into the Reply Window text box, and sign your name or screen name at the end.

5. To send a copy of your reply to the original poster's e-mail box, check Send via e-mail at the top of the Reply window. To add your reply to the message board, make sure the Post to message board box is checked.

6. Click Send and your message proudly goes on its way.

Figure 8-3: Use the Quote button to copy the original poster's text in a message board posting.

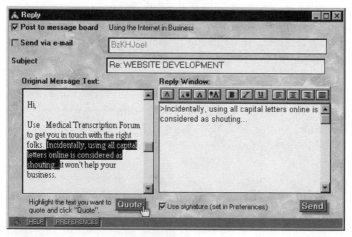

Although you can disagree with what others say in the message boards, you can't tell them they have no right to say it. Remember what mom always said: Be nice and play fair. That goes for the message boards, too. Losing your temper and screaming at someone in a message board or e-mail is known as *flaming*. Flaming somebody qualifies as another of those activities that the AOL Cops don't like.

CHAPTER 9

CRUISING THE WEB

IN THIS CHAPTER

- Learning the Ins and Outs of the AOL Web browser
- Viewing a friend's Web site
- Using the Web to see the world

People love the Web. They love the flashiness of the graphics, the hyperlinks that take you from site to site with a click of the mouse, and the information gleaned from a few minutes' searching. If you're using a slow modem, however, the Web certainly earns its nickname of "World Wide Wait." On the other hand, if you have a quick modem (more than 28,800 bps), the Web reveals all kinds of virtual treasures — if you know how to find them.

Browsing through the Internet

America Online uses Microsoft Internet Explorer as its built-in Web browser. After you *load* a Web page (so that the Web page appears on-screen), you can use your mouse to move from one article or section to another or even from Web page to Web page (see Figure 9-1). Any time that the mouse cursor turns into a hand, that button, link, or image is fair game. Click it to open another portion of the Web site or jump to an entirely different site.

Figure 9-1: AOL's Web site appears, with loads of links ripe for clicking.

Because of the integration between the AOL software and the browser, members don't notice a huge difference if they enter a keyword that opens a Web site rather than an area that AOL stores on its system. Of course, if you do enter such a keyword, the AOL Web browser opens instead of a little window. But no large warning box appears stating, "Wait! I'm searching for a Web page now!" Instead, the browser window quietly appears, and the page loads into the browser just as all the other online windows do.

Use the buttons at the top of the AOL browser bar to navigate from Web site to Web site. Table 9-1 shows you what these buttons mean (they go from left to right).

Table 9-1   AOL Browser Buttons

Name	Looks Like	What It Does
Previous	An arrow pointing to the left	Looks at the last window you saw — possibly a Web page or an AOL forum window.
Next	An arrow pointing to the right	Takes you forward to the window you were visiting before clicking Previous.
Stop	A circle with an X in it	Stops loading a Web page.
Reload	An arrow curved to look like a circle	Tells the browser to try loading the page again. Use this button if something goes wrong while accessing a Web site.
Home	A house	Loads the Web page you specify as your home page — generally, www.aol.com, America Online's official home page.

Tip

Even America Online keywords take you to Web sites these days. Don't be surprised to see the Web browser open if you click a link in an area or enter a keyword into the keyword dialog box. You may see the full browser or just a small browser window (such as the one shown in Figure 9-2), which is about the size of the AOL Welcome window.

Figure 9-2: Online areas often incorporate small browser windows such as this one.

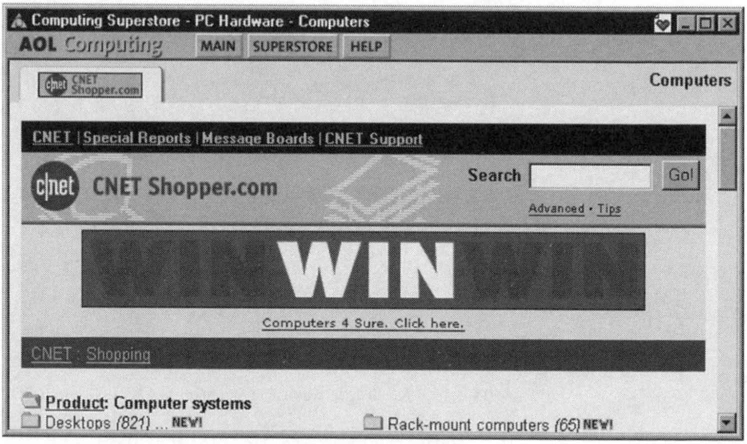

Using Web Site Addresses

You see them everywhere these days: www.yahoo.com, www.whitehouse.gov, or www.idgbooks.com — even the local grocery store proudly plasters its Web-site address on every paper bag you carry home. Sometimes these strange looking codes begin with http://. Other times they simply start with www. What's the deal?

HTTP (or *http*, as you often see it written) stands for *H*yper-*T*ext *T*ransport *P*rotocol — a fancy way of saying, "Hey! I have Web text here." Not too long ago, Web surfers needed to type the http:// into the Web browser's text field; otherwise, the browser had no idea what to do. Thankfully, Web browsers are a lot smarter these days. Now they automatically know to place the http:// in front of any address that begins www, and folks who surf the Net are grateful.

The browser bar shown in Figure 9-3 provides a handy way to connect to Web sites. Type the Web-site address into the browser bar's text box and click Go. The browser window opens, and the page you requested begins to load. Well, that's what happens most of the time. Sometimes, however, Web sites don't function correctly, a glitch comes down the phone wire along with the computer code, or some other flaky things happen, and the Web site freezes halfway to your screen. When that sort of thing happens, click Go again or click the Reload button to see whether that fixes the problem.

Figure 9-3:   Type the Web address and give it a Go.

See a Friend's Site at Hometown AOL

Hometown AOL, America Online's member Web-site area, showcases the Web sites created by AOL members. Members create a Web page and then upload it to Hometown AOL so that other members (and people on the Net) can see them. Here's how to check out Hometown AOL:

■ Use keyword: **Hometown AOL** to open the Welcome to Hometown AOL page, as shown in Figure 9-4.

■ Visit a friend's Web site by typing the friend's screen name into the Search Pages text box and clicking the Search button.

■ Browse through the categories in the Explore Member Pages area by clicking any links that look interesting.

Figure 9-4: Explore AOL members' Web pages through Hometown AOL.

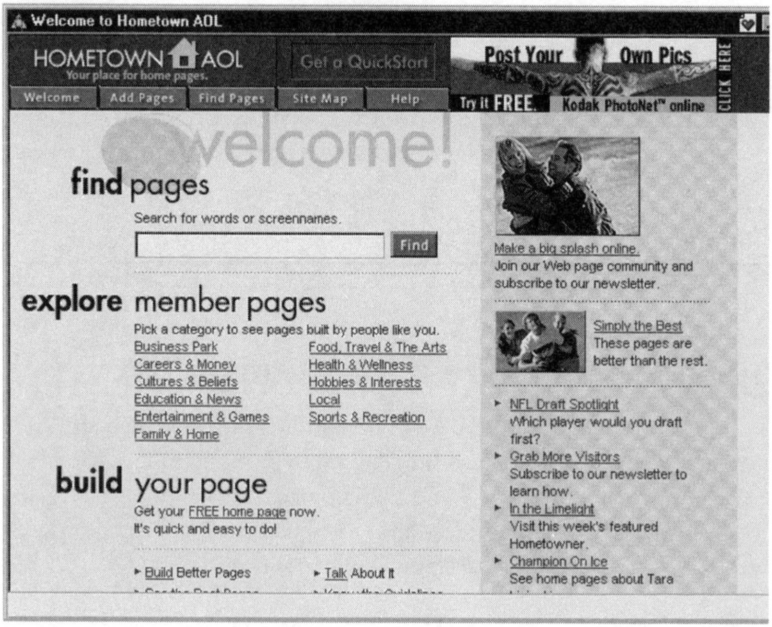

America Online divides Hometown AOL Web pages into categories for education, entertainment, family, food, health, hobbies, and sports, to name just a few. If you want to find a business site that an AOL member maintains, look in Hometown AOL's Business Park.

Use the Find Pages text box to search for specific topics or for screen names in Hometown AOL.

Travel the World with Web Sites

After you have access to the Internet, you can see the world without ever leaving your computer. From Web-based news articles written in foreign languages to Web sites devoted to particular countries, the world's marvels await you. You can also use the Web to help research an actual vacation, whether you're planning on visiting the next state or halfway around the world.

Use the Web to see the world

Even if you don't plan to visit soon, the Web offers information on virtually every country in the world. Whether you harbor an armchair interest in a particular country or you actually dream of visiting someday, look to Web sites for statistic, news, and social tips. To research a country through your Web browser, follow these steps:

1. Type **netfind.com** into the browser bar text field and click the Go button. AOL NetFind opens, ready to conduct your search.

2. Enter the country's name into the Search text box, and click Search. AOL NetFind then presents you with a list of possible matches for your country (see Figure 9-5).

3. Browse through the hyperlinks and descriptions, clicking any entry that looks promising. The top of the results page lists links for weather, general information, and travel.

Figure 9-5:   Research a country's statistics or customs through the Web.

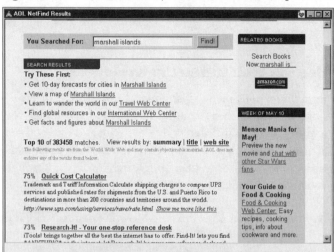

Depending on the information you want, you can narrow the search by including more specific terms:

■   Use the word **news** after the country name in the search text box to get current international events, as well as links to online news articles in that country's native language or English.

■   Insert a word like **culture** or **social** in front of the country name in the search text box. The search should return links for research results or sites that specialize in that country's cultural history or present norms.

■   On your initial search, mark the best sites as Favorite Places. Then, when you have time, use your Favorite Places list to browse through each of these favorites to locate the specific details you need.

Web information abounds for travelers

Before you hop on a plane that's bound for some distant airport, take some time to research your trip on the Web. You

can find everything from destinations to sightseeing suggestions. After you've decided on a vacation decision, use the
Web to book a flight, reserve a hotel, or purchase an entire
travel package.

Here's how to research a potential vacation via the Web:

1. Type www.previewtravel.com into the AOL
browser bar text field and click the Go button.

2. Use the Destination Guides button to see a page with
three possible destination categories: US, including
Hawaii, Mexico, and the Caribbean and More International Destinations.

3. Click on the arrow next to one of the three selections to
see a drop-down list; then highlight any possible destination from the list and click the Go button.

4. The Destination Guide opens, full of articles about that
particular spot's activities, accommodations, and assets
(see Figure 9-6).

Figure 9-6:   Destination Guides abound with useful travel information.

5. Click on any of the links along the left hand side of the city's destination page. These links lead to information about dining, hotels, attractions, and visitor-friendly tips.

6. If you decide you want to see another destination, use the Previous arrow on the browser bar to return to the Destination Guides main page and select another city from the lists.

7. You can make reservations directly through the Preview Travel site. If you prefer to compare prices, try entering Internet Air Fares (`www.air-fare.com`) into the browser bar. Click the Go button to retrieve the Internet Air Fares page. Internet Air Fares compares fares between airlines to give you the lowest rate they can.

Whether or not you drive to your vacation destination, you may want a map to help you become familiar with new territory. MapQuest (`www.mapquest.com`) provides maps of United States and worldwide destinations that you can view on-screen or print from your printer. Along with the map, MapQuest offers free door-to-door directions if you're the type of driver who navigates better with written directions (see Figure 9-7). To view a city's map, click the Maps hyperlink in the main MapQuest page. For driving maps and directions, click the Driving Directions hyperlink.

MapQuest also includes a travel guide that gives you a little information about the city along with a great map. To use MapQuest's travel information, follow these steps:

1. Type **www.mapquest.com** into the browser bar and click the Go button. The Mapquest site opens in the browser window.

2. Click the Travel Guide link on the main MapQuest page. A Travel Guide page opens, containing text boxes and buttons along the right-hand side.

Figure 9-7:   View or print travel maps with MapQuest.

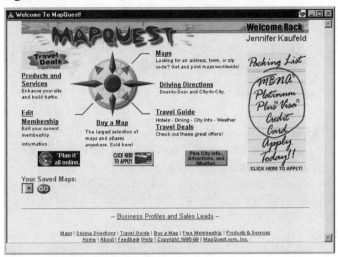

3. Type the address, if you know it, into the Address text box.

4. Type your destination city into the City text box, and the state into the State text box.

5. If you know the zip code, you can include it in the Zip text box; the code is not necessary if you enter the city and state.

6. Now use the buttons below the text boxes to tell MapQuest what you want to know. Choices include Lodging, Dining, City Info, Weather, and Itinerary. MapQuest then presents you with a form to fill out (if you want dining or hotel information), a map and general information (for city info), or they redirect your request to a weather site for weather information. In order to use the MapQuest Itinerary feature, you need to register with MapQuest.

7. MapQuest asks you to verify where you want to go by clicking the hyperlink it provides, and then the site shows you its information. Once you find a hotel or restaurant you like, you can add it to a trip itinerary.

8. Click the Add to Itinerary button in the top right-hand corner of the information window to add the chosen hotel(s) and restaurants to your trip schedule. MapQuest asks if you want to add the information to an itinerary for the city name you're researching; click the OK button to place the lodging or dining details in your online itinerary.

To use MapQuest's Itinerary feature, you need to register with the site. Registration with MapQuest is free, and it gives you a unique Web site address you can use to research trips and save travel plans. To register with MapQuest, follow these steps:

1. Register with MapQuest by clicking the Free Membership button on the main MapQuest page. A Free Membership screen appears, listing the benefits of MapQuest membership.

2. Scroll to the bottom of the Free Membership page and enter your name and e-mail address (`screen name@aol.com`) into the text boxes.

3. Click Join Now. MapQuest then shows you a screen welcoming you as a member. In the middle of the page, you'll see a long hyperlink listed under the words `Your Personal URL is`.

4. Highlight the entire hyperlink, copy it, and paste it into the browser bar.

5. Click the Go button. MapQuest then shows you its main page, along with a friendly Welcome Back icon in the upper-right corner.

6. Click the Favorite Places button in the upper-right corner of the browser window to mark this page as a favorite place. You need to use this personalized page if you want MapQuest to give you destination itineraries.

7. Close the browser by clicking the close button in the upper-right corner of the browser window.

8. Click Favorites on the toolbar, and then click the MapQuest Membership entry at the bottom of the drop-down list that appears. Your personal MapQuest page loads, ready to store your travel plans.

CHAPTER 10

DOIN' FUN STUFF

IN THIS CHAPTER

- Finding hobbies online
- Reading the fun news areas
- Locating movie information

Make your online romps more interesting by visiting a few less-traveled areas online. Although you can eventually find most of what you need through the Channels window, many of the sites listed in this chapter may take you a while to locate — they're usually tucked into the dim corners of out-of-the-way windows. View this list as a tiny representation of the forums available and remember to click any folder icon that looks interesting as you surf. You may unearth other gems similar to the ones that I describe in this chapter.

Business

If business or work questions nag, you can always turn to America Online for resources and support. The WorkPlace channel contains loads of great resources and forums. Those areas that I list in the following sections are especially helpful in what they provide.

Business Know-How

You can increase your business if you have the right knowledge. *Business Know-How* (keyword: **Business Know-How**) gives you tips on marketing, home businesses, human resources, small businesses, and lots of other topics. Also look here for scheduled chats for people in all lines of work as well as strategies for marketing, creating business plans, or starting a business.

Business Travel

The *Global Citizen's International Business Etiquette* area (keyword: **Global Citizen**) is great reading even if you're only dreaming about visiting a particular place. Its window sports an item list of culture tips for various countries that's specifically designed with the business traveler in mind. From Mexico to Thailand, this area makes good research before a trip.

Business Week Online

Keep up with business news and features with *Business Week Online* (keyword: **BW**). Read current stories or research the past four weeks' archives. Check out *BW Daily* for daily news and articles arranged by column title or *BW Plus* for articles arranged by topic, such as computing, small business, or women and business.

Career Center

Thinking of changing careers or simply branching out? Drop into the *Career Center* (keyword: **Career Center**) for a nudge in the right direction (see Figure 10-1). This area lists forums for a huge number of professions as well as buttons that lead to job-hunting help, online courses, and a salary calculator.

Company News

Company News (keyword: **Company News**) lets you search the Reuters and Business Wire article reserve for stories on any company as long as you know its ticker symbol. The search returns stories by date, beginning with the most recent. Don't know the company's ticker symbol? Click Look Up Ticker at the bottom of the window and use the Lookup search system to find the right symbol.

Figure 10-1: Enhance your career with help from the Career Center.

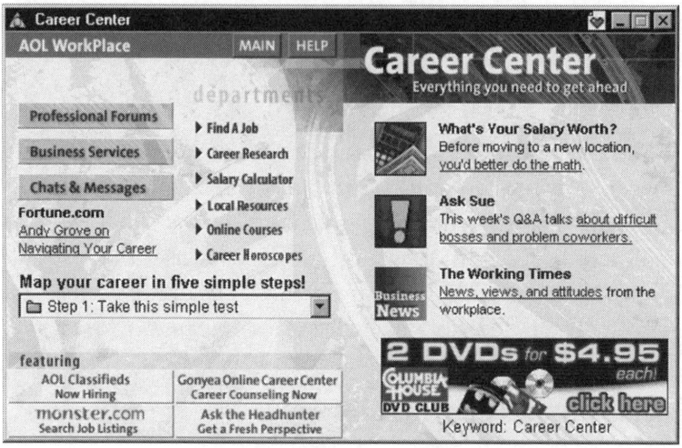

E-mail Finder

Looking for someone's e-mail address? Try *E-mail Finder* (keyword: **Email Finder**). Keep in mind, however, that not all e-mail search systems cover everyone's e-mail address, and many addresses you find may be out of date — especially as often as some people change providers. (The best way to learn someone's e-mail address is to pick up the phone and call the person.)

Link Exchange

Advertise your business Web site for free at *Link Exchange* (keyword: **Link Exchange**). You agree to place links to other people's sites on your Web page, and someone in turn (maybe a lot of someones) use your business link on their site.

Hobbies

Although the Interests channel highlights a massive number of hobbies, the channel misses one here and there. Check the following sections for some interesting forums that may (or

may not) have listings in the Interests channel. Use keyword:
Hobbies to visit the main hobby window online and mouse
around from there.

Camping

Look to *Backpacker Magazine* Online (keyword: **Camping**)
for camping and trail information (see Figure 10-2). The area
offers discussion boards and a chat room, articles from *Backpacker Magazine*, and information on a myriad of products
of interest to backpackers and campers.

Figure 10-2:   Get gear tips and camping information from Backpacker Magazine
Online.

Outdoor Adventure Online (keyword: **OAO**) also contains
some camping information, such as a link to CampUSA, a
campground directory. Outdoor Adventure Online, however,
is primarily geared to adventure vacations, such as whitewa-
ter rafting.

Collecting

The Collecting forum (keyword: **Collecting**) covers most collectibles from Beanie Babies to Antiques. Select a folder from the list and read messages, tour Web sites, and swap tips with other collectors.

The keyword **Gaming** takes you to a window featuring Collectible Card Games, or CCGs. Trade with other CCG fanatics, attend a scheduled chat, or drop into a chat room to find out how to assemble a deck (assuming, of course, that you want to *play* with the cards you collect).

Crafts

Keyword **Crafts** transports you to the Crafts forum, where you can create anything imaginable (or at least read about it). Look here for links to message boards on crochet, cross stitch, jewelry, knitting, needlecraft, paper crafts, polymer clay, pottery, sewing, stained glass, weaving, woodworking, and more. You can also use the link in this area to jump to the Craft Corner, AOL U.K.'s craft area.

Turn to Woman's Day Online (keyword: **WD**) for a list of craft ideas, from decorating to knitting. Each craft idea includes downloadable instructions so that you can make it yourself.

Family Life Online's Projects area (keyword: **Family Life**) lists several crafts that you can make with the kids, from homemade tinkertoys to gift ideas. Look through the list box for an interesting idea, download the instructions, and have a ball.

Movies

In addition to the Entertainment channel, several movie areas online offer additional reviews and movie info. Check them out.

Home Video

At Home Video (keyword: **Home Video**), you can locate a particular video or read a movie's review. You can even purchase videos and DVDs online from this window or view a list of new video releases.

MovieLink

MovieLink (keyword: **MovieLink**) tells you what shows are playing when (see Figure 10-3). Tell the site what city you're in, and it tells you where you can see the show and what time the movie begins. MovieLink's a great resource for travelers with a free evening or two and also saves time for moviegoers at home.

Figure 10-3:   Find that new flick's show times with MovieLink.

Movies on the Web

Use Movies on the Web (keyword: **Movies Web**) to link to many different movie-related sites, from movie ratings to box-office statistics. When you find a site or two that you really like, use the Favorite Places feature to bookmark the site so that you can find it again easily.

News

Turn to the News channel for top stories, or visit one of the following other areas for articles that are both interesting and unique.

Chicago Tribune

The *Trib* (keyword: **Tribune**) can keep you current on news and opinion, Chicago style. The department buttons down the side of the window cover many of the *Tribune's* sections; for a complete list (including the crossword puzzle and Jumble) click the Site Index button.

Extra Online

Extra Online (keyword: **Extra**) brings you news focusing on the entertainment industry. If you itch to know more about a celebrity or you want coverage of movies or television, *Extra Online* fits the bill.

International News

Read news from around the world! For true international flavor, open the Foreign Newspapers folder in the *International News* window (keyword: **Intl News**). Browse by continent and then by country and read news from its international source. This area is useful if you study a foreign language, because many of these newspapers appear in their home tongues.

It's a Mad, Mad World

Jump on this merry-go-round for the wacky news (keyword: **Mad World**). Guaranteed to bring a chuckle or a shake of the head, these news stories border on the bizarre. Ranging from strange items on the news wires to political cartoons, *It's a Mad, Mad World* is a must-see if you like to laugh.

News Search

Look for the news stories that you want to read with *News Search* (keyword: **News Search**). Enter the word or words you want AOL to search for. Then click List Articles, and the results window fills with stories. Whether you receive a few or a lot or articles depends on your subject and how many stories have filtered through the news services in the past 30 days.

Stocks

For basic stock information as well as investment basics, turn to the *Personal Finance* channel (keyword: **Personal Finance**). Full of opinions, tips, and informative articles, Personal Finance provides a wealth of resources for the person interested in investments.

The Motley Fool

For a lighthearted look at the stock market, visit *The Motley Fool: Finance and Folly* forum (keyword: **Fool**), as shown in Figure 10-4. The Motley Fool offers a Fool's School to teach the basics of stocks and investments, Nine Nightly Stops in Fooldom to remind you of the online areas to check frequently to keep up to date on investing news, and an *excellent* article about the potential dangers of believing everything that you read online — Read This First: Investing Online. It's worth a gander.

Figure 10-4: Learn stock market investing from The Motley Fool.

Quotes

Quotes (keyword: **Quotes**) lets you enter any ticker symbol and receive near-current trading information. Because the results hit AOL's system (and consequently, your screen) 25 minutes or more after they're posted, you probably don't want to trade on the information you read here. Consider it for information only and call your broker if you want to actually invest money.

Sports

Have a favorite team? Try the team name (or nickname) as a keyword. More than likely, a window appears on-screen with that team's schedule, roster, statistics, and a links to a few news stories.

Use your favorite sport as a keyword: **Auto Racing**, **Horse Sports**, **Baseball**, **Football**, and **Soccer** all open various windows dedicated to those sports. Many others do, too. Think of a sport and try it as a keyword. How about **Lacrosse**?

The keyword **Sports Trivia** opens the NTN Sports Trivia window. Whether you enjoy hockey, football, basketball, baseball, the Olympics, or general sports, NTN offers a trivia game for you. But watch out . . . these trivia games are addictive. You may find yourself spending an entire evening answering questions and watching your ranking rise and fall. (Good thing it's free.)

Software

Each day, the AOL computing gurus select a cool file that members can download — for free (keyword: **Daily Download**). Of course, it may not be anything you're interested in — downloads range from the truly techie to files for the masses.

Use the keyword: **Download Software** to open AOL Computing's Download Software window. Divided into shareware and retail software by tabs at the top of an item list, *shareware* is software that you can download for free and *retail* is software that you download (and pay for) instead of going to the computer store and buying it there. The Download Software window generally opens with an active Shareware file tab; browse the folders of downloadable files and download those that sound intriguing.

Travel Planning

Make the *Travel* channel a first stop on the travel-planning agenda. Full of reservation help and vacation ideas, the channel is dedicated to helping members find what they need. If you can't find what you're looking for, however, or if you want something a little different, try one of the following travel areas.

Destination Guides

Decide whether you want to visit a major city or a whole new country, and send *Destination Guides* (keyword: **Destinations**) on a search to see what it can find. When the city's window opens, it shows an introduction to the city, plus links for sights to see, places to stay, restaurant reviews, current weather, the best time to visit — in short, more information than you can use even in a two-week stay. Figure 10-5 shows the Destination Guides window.

Figure 10-5:   Pick a vacation destination, and let Destination Guides tell you all about it.

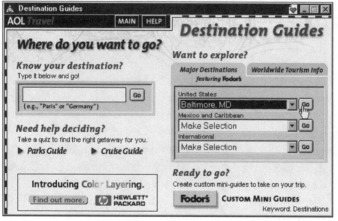

International Travel

Research that international trip, including help for taking AOL on the road, with *International Travel* (keyword: **Intl Travel**). Learn about other cultures and read up on etiquette tips. Looking for resources on everything from guidebooks to international money? Check out the Planning & Preparation folder.

Weather

Keyword **Weather** opens the AOL Weather Center, complete with today's forecast. Enter a city name and click Search for that area's detailed and extended forecast, and you can plan your day accordingly. The Weather Center is very useful if you plan to visit a different area of the country.

Hurricane Survival Guide

Get important hurricane information from AOL's *Hurricane Survival Guide* (keyword: **OSO Storm**). Offering information in categories ranging all the way from *Anticipating the Storm* to *Returning to Normal*, this window provides excellent help for members who live in hurricane regions — or students researching hurricanes for school.

Worldwide Weather

Use the keyword **Intl Weather** to check the forecasts for the U.K., Germany, Canada, and France, as well as to get other world-weather predictions. Whether you plan to travel to one of these countries, you have friends or family there, or you're simply curious, *Worldwide Weather* offers forecasts for tropical climates, the snow-covered Alps, and everything in between.

WSC Weather Mall

Looking for a wind chime, bird house, or sundial? The *WSC Weather Mall* (keyword: **Weather Mall**) carries barometers, bat houses, cloud charts, jigsaw puzzles, books, videos, hats, umbrellas — even a weather-inspired necktie! If it's about weather, you should find it somewhere in this online store.

CLIFFSNOTES REVIEW

Use this CliffsNotes Review to practice what you've learned in this book and to build your confidence in doing the job right the first time. After you work through the review questions, the problem-solving exercises, and the visual test, you're well on your way to achieving your goal of going online with AOL.

Q&A

1. The Quotes button on the toolbar:

   a. Gives you a "Quote of the Day."

   b. Lets you send thoughts to AOL staff

   c. Takes you to the Stock Quotes window

2. Where do you look for the Switch Screen Names command?

_____

3. Assuming your screen name is Boss302, what e-mail address do you give to a friend who's not a member of AOL to send you Internet e-mail?

   a. boss302@aol.com

   b. Boss302@AmericaOnline.com

   c. Boss302

4. How do you open the Write Mail window in one easy step?

_____

5. Which is false about computer viruses?

   a. You can contract a virus simply by opening an e-mail message.

   b. A virus could appear as an e-mail attachment that you download into your computer.

   c. Some viruses cause a lot of computer damage, others don't.

6. Name two ways you can open the Keyword dialog box.

_____

7. Which keyword takes you to the software libraries on AOL?

   a. Download Software

   b. Software4U

   c. Software Store

8. What keyword takes you to AOL's large scheduled chat area?

   a. Scheduled Chats

   b. AOL Live

   c. Live Guests

9. Which channel did AOL specifically design for youngsters?

_____

_____

10. Flaming is

   a. against Terms of Service

   b. replying angrily to a discussion board post

   c. both of the above

Answers: (1) c. (2) Under the Sign Off menu bar item. (3) a. (4) Click the Write button on the toolbar. (5) a. (6) Click the keyword button on browser bar; use the Favorites toolbar button and then click Go to Keyword. (7) a. (8) b. (9) Kids Only. (10) c.

Scenarios

1. You receive an Instant Message from someone you don't know and, after a few friendly exchanges, the other person begins to type foul language into the Instant Message window. You politely ask them to stop, but the abusive language continues. You should

_____

2. A message arrives in your e-mail box from an address you never heard of, and a subject that says "Hi, remember me?" The blue disk icon next to the subject tells you that the sender attached a file of some kind to the message. To be safe, you

_____

3. You find an online area you think an AOL friend will love. To let her know about it, you send it to her in an e-mail message by

_____

Answers: (1) Click Notify AOL on the Instant Message window. (2) Highlight the message and click Delete. (3) Clicking the Favorite Places icon and choosing Insert in Mail.

Visual Test

1.

| Find ▾ | Type Keyword or Web Address here and click Go | ▾ |

Type a keyword here to go to an _____ _____. Type a Web address to go to the_____.

2. Which of these icons indicates the type of e-mail message that *could* carry a virus?

a. ▣

b. ▣

Answers: (1) AOL department; Internet. (2) b.

Consider This

- Did you know that you can use AOL as your online newspaper and get all your breaking news, plus slide shows, from the News channel?

- Did you know you can send e-mail to all your friends at once by using the New Group button in the Address Book to create one big entry with everyone in it? Save time sending out that family newsletter.

- Did you know that you can create a Web page for your business for free with your AOL account and post it in Hometown

AOL's Business Park for others to see?

Practice Projects

1. Create another screen name under your account. Send an e-mail from the new screen name to your other screen name.

2. Send an attached file to your original screen name and then sign on with your original screen name and download the file.

3. Find an area you really like and send its Favorite Place link your other screen name in an e-mail message.

4. Change the parental controls on the new screen name. Then sign onto the system with the screen name and see what the controls allow you to do.

5. Use a Web search system like AOL Netfind to research a favorite topic. Mark all the useful sites you find as Favorite Places so that you can show them to a friend later.

CLIFFSNOTES RESOURCE CENTER

After you're comfortable with the material in this book, you're ready to take the next step in the online world. In this Cliffs Notes Resource Center, we've anticipated some places that you may want to explore next. Here, you'll find the best of the best — links to the best information in print and online about AOL and online communities.

Books

This CliffsNotes book is one of the many great books about the online world published by IDG Books Worldwide, Inc. So if you want some great books to help you continue your journey, check out some of these publications:

America Online For Dummies, 5th Edition. John Kaufeld gives tips and tricks for getting the most out of America Online in a book that doesn't take itself too seriously. If you're the type person who wants more depth in the topic but who doesn't feel guilty about enjoying the learning process, then this is the book for you. IDG Books Worldwide, $19.99.

The Internet and the World Wide Web Simplified, 3rd Edition. Some people absorb material most efficiently by seeing it presented graphically. If you're this type of person, then your best bet for learning more about the Internet is this informative, full-color guide to using and cruising the Internet. Read less; learn more. IDG Books Worldwide, $24.99.

Creating Web Pages For Dummies, 4th Edition. After checking out other AOL members' Web Pages, you just may decide that you want join the online publishing revolution, too. Chapter 5 of this book by Bud Smith and Arthur Bebak explains creating Web pages specifically with AOL, and if your interested in using FrontPage Express to create your Web page, you're covered. IDG Books Worldwide, $24.99.

Genealogy Online For Dummies. Genealogy is all the rage these days, and with good reason: The power of the Internet makes it easier than ever to find out where you come from and what your ancestors accomplished. Find out how in this book by Matthew and April Leigh Helm. IDG Books Worldwide, $24.99.

CliffsNotes Investing in the Stock Market. AOL has some really good resources for first-time investors, but investing in the stock market for the first time can be a frightening proposition. Why not take the CliffsNotes road to learning about the stock market and choosing securities? Whether you want to invest real money or just "play," this CliffsNotes book by Mercedes Bailey brings you what you need to know about the stock market. IDG Books Worldwide. $8.99.

It's easy to find books published by IDG Books Worldwide. You can find them in your favorite online and traditional bookstores. You can also check out the following Web sites:

- `www.cliffsnotes.com`
- `www.dummies.com`
- `www.idgbooks.com`

Internet

Check out these Web sites for more information about your PC—buying, using, upgrading, and more.

Bluemountain, `www.bluemountain.com` Forget a birthday or anniversary? Well, bluemountain is the Web's most popular site for sending greeting cards online. And it's free!

Yahoo!, www.yahoo.com Yahoo! is one of the great *portals* to the Internet (those places where you just naturally go to get started). Whether you're searching for particular information or just want to chat with friends, Yahoo! is a terrific place to point your browser.

CNN, www.cnn.com CNN is a great Web site to check out up-to-the-moment news and breaking stories both in the United States and Internationally. CNN also has large areas that cover sports, financial news, entertainment news, and more.

Download.com, www.download.com If you're looking for a particular shareware or freeware program to run on your PC, chances are good that download.com has what you're looking for. Check out their featured downloads or you can use a keyword search to locate the program you seek.

Next time you're on the Internet, don't forget to drop by www.cliffsnotes.com. There, you'll find a Resource Center that you can use today, tomorrow, and beyond.

Send Us Your Favorite Tips

In your quest for learning, have you ever experienced that sublime moment when you figure out a trick that saves time or trouble? Perhaps you realized you were taking ten steps to accomplish something that could have taken two. Or you've found a little-known workaround that gets great results. If you've discovered a useful tip that helped you use AOL more effectively, and you'd like to share it, we'd love to hear from you. Go to our Web site at www.cliffsnotes.com and look for the Talk to Us button. If your tip is selected, we may publish it as part of CliffsNotes Daily, our exciting free email newsletter. To find out more, or to subscribe to a newsletter, go to on the Web.

INDEX

T

U

V

W

Y

COMING SOON FROM CLIFFSNOTES

Online Shopping

HTML

Choosing a PC

Beginning Programming

Careers

Windows 98 Home Networking

eBay Online Auctions

PC Upgrade and Repair

Business

Microsoft Word 2000

Microsoft PowerPoint 2000

Finance

Microsoft Outlook 2000

Digital Photography

Palm Computing

Investing

Windows 2000

Online Research

IDG
BOOKS
WORLDWIDE

COMING SOON FROM CLIFFSNOTES
Buying and Selling on eBay

Have you ever experienced the thrill of finding an incredible bargain at a specialty store or been amazed at what people are willing to pay for things that you might toss in the garbage? If so, then you'll want to learn about eBay — the hottest auction site on the Internet. And CliffsNotes *Buying and Selling on eBay* is the shortest distance to eBay proficiency. You'll learn how to:

- Find what you're looking for, from antique toys to classic cars

- Watch the auctions strategically and place bids at the right time

- Sell items online at the eBay site

- Make the items you sell attractive to prospective bidders

- Protect yourself from fraud

Here's an example of how the step-by-step CliffsNotes learning process simplifies placing a bid at eBay:

1. Scroll to the Web page form that is located at the bottom of the page on which the auction item itself is presented.

2. Enter your registered eBay username and password and enter the amount you want to bid. A Web page appears that lets you review your bid before you actually submit it to eBay. After you're satisfied with your bid, click the Place Bid button.

3. Click the Back button on your browser until you return to the auction listing page. Then choose View⇨Reload (Netscape Navigator) or View⇨Refresh (Microsoft Internet Explorer) to reload the Web page information. Your new high bid appears on the Web page, and your name appears as the high bidder.

W9-CZV-588

The Mysterious House Number Nine

By John Parker

Illustrated by Clive Spong

DOMINIE PRESS

Pearson Learning Group

Publisher: Raymond Yuen
Project Editor: John S. F. Graham
Editor: Bob Rowland
Designer: Greg DiGenti
Illustrator: Clive Spong

Text Copyright © 2003 John Parker
Illustrations Copyright © 2003 Dominie Press, Inc.
All rights reserved. No part of this publication may
be reproduced or transmitted in any form or by any
means without permission in writing from the publisher.
Reproduction of any part of this book, through photocopy,
recording, or any electronic or mechanical retrieval system,
without the written permission of the publisher, is an
infringement of the copyright law.

Published by:

🔴 **Dominie Press, Inc.**

1949 Kellogg Avenue
Carlsbad, California 92008 USA

www.dominie.com

1-800-232-4570

Paperback ISBN 0-7685-1627-7
Printed in Singapore by PH Productions Pte Ltd
    2 3 4 5 6 PH 05

Table of Contents

Chapter One
The Old House

When we moved into our new neighborhood, all the houses were neat and clean—except number nine.

Number nine was a mess. The grass was long. The hedge was overgrown. The mailbox had fallen over. I think the only thing holding up the roof was the rust.

The curtains sagged. So did one of the windows. And the paint was peeling. The house looked empty.

Mom told me there was a Mr. Shaw living there. He didn't like talking to people—and he owned a big dog.

One day, as I walked down the sidewalk in front of the house, I decided to stop and take a look. The front yard was fenced in, and there was a gate leading to a walkway.

I didn't see a dog anywhere. I thought maybe Mom was wrong. Maybe there was no dog and no Mr. Shaw.

I decided to push the front gate open.

It creaked loudly on rusty hinges. All of a sudden, I heard a bark come from nowhere. Then I saw a huge dog at the window of the old house.

It stared at me with hungry yellow eyes, and its bark rumbled through the house. I took off back up the street.

That night I dreamed about number nine. I dreamed I was walking past the house, when the huge dog leaped at me from under the hedge. It grabbed my shoe in its iron jaws. Then Mr. Shaw came out—with a paper bag over his head. He was feeling for the steps with his feet, and holding his arms out. On the second step he tripped and fell into the long grass.

"Help me, dog!" he yelled.

The dog bit my shoe even harder. I tried to shake him off.

Then I woke up, shivering and shaking. All my blankets were in a heap on the floor.

I was glad it was only a dream.

Chapter Two
Smoke!

Usually, I like school, but the next day
I didn't pay much attention. Miss
Marbeck pointed this out to me twice.

"Stop daydreaming, Troy," she said.

But I couldn't stop daydreaming.

I kept wondering what Mr. Shaw looked

like. What did he do for a living? What kind of a person was he?

He could have been anything. He could have been Mr. Bad-Tempered Shaw. He might have black eyebrows and a scowl.

"Buzz off," he'd growl, "or I'll put the dog on you."

He could have been Mr. Cat-Burglar Shaw. That's why he had to stay inside all day, hiding all the things he had stolen. Then he would go out at night to steal more stuff. He would have a ski mask and a black cat burglar outfit, plus a big flashlight for lighting up dark rooms.

He could have been Mr. Mad Scientist Shaw, working on a secret invention. Nobody would guess that inside his run-down old house was a huge laboratory.

Test tubes would bubble. Lights and

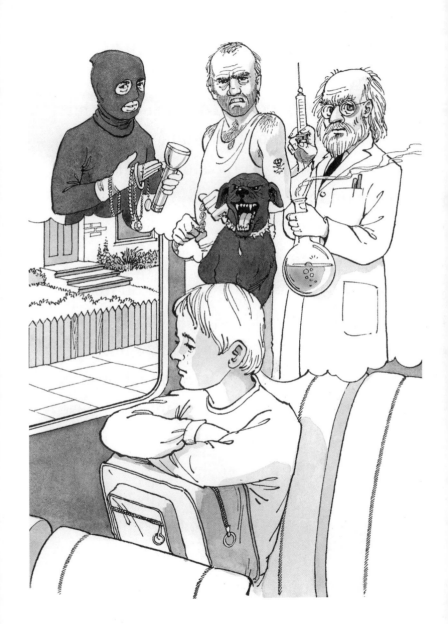

panels would flash and whirr. The big dog would growl at the rats in their cages.

I thought about it so much in the bus on the way home that I almost missed my stop. I pressed the stop bar just in time and practically ran to the front of the bus to get off. The bus driver had to brake so hard that I landed in the lap of an elderly woman and spilled all her apples out of her shopping bag!

After I helped her pick them up, I stepped off the bus. Mr. Shaw's house was between the bus stop and my house. I couldn't help looking at number nine as I walked by.

Then I saw something really strange. Smoke was coming out of the chimney.

Why would anyone light a fire on such a warm afternoon? I watched for two to three minutes, until the smoke stopped.

During dinner I asked Mom about it.

"There are a lot of trees that shade his house," Mom said. "It could be cold inside. Maybe he lit the fire because his heater isn't working."

That didn't make sense to me. I thought of a better reason.

Mr. Shaw was burning trash in his fireplace because he knew that people would see him if he burned trash out in the open. They would report him to the police. But he's too smart for that.

I went to have another look. I don't know why, but I decided to open the gate again. I was careful not to let it creak. Number nine looked as empty as ever—until I saw the dog in the window. Its yellow eyes were like saucers.

Then the dog did something that made my heart hammer with shock. The window was slightly open. The dog stuck its nose in the gap, sniffed a little, and pushed its way further out. Then it pushed the window up with its head, making a terrible cracking, creaking noise.

I stopped dead in my tracks. The dog started barking wildly. It leaped out of the window and headed right for me.

Chapter Three
Going Inside

My legs moved so fast, they almost came off! I imagined the dog's sharp teeth about to rip into me. My heart pounded. My lungs felt dry—but it didn't happen. The dog was much faster than I was, but it didn't catch me. Then from

behind me I heard a whine.

I stopped running and looked back. The dog whined again.

I took a step toward it, and it wagged its tail. Maybe it was happy because I was its next meal!

I took a step away—it whined. Another step closer—and that big black tail wagged again.

I came even closer to the dog, slowly coming up to it. Then I saw that its nose was bleeding, most likely from the window.

I managed to say, "G-g-good dog," through my fear.

Then it turned and galloped up to the front door of number nine. It looked at me and whined.

I got the message—the dog wanted me to go inside!

I really didn't want to go into number nine. Maybe Mr. Mad Scientist Shaw was waiting inside the front door. He could have been waiting there, about to hit me over the head and use me in an experiment.

Maybe he would make me swallow something horrible that would turn me into a space alien or something.

I gulped and tiptoed onto the landing at the top of the steps. *OUCH!* I heard a crunching sound and felt my leg fall through the porch, right through a rotten board. The cracked wood scraped my skin—but I tried hard not to cry out. What if Mr. Shaw was listening, ready to grab me?

The dog came over. I thought it was going to eat my leg—but it just licked my wound. Then it waited by the front door, whining at me. The dog's tail wagged as I put my hand on the doorknob.

My heart was racing. What would happen?

I turned the knob. It moved, so the door wasn't locked. But the door wouldn't open.

I pushed again while the dog whined and scratched to get in. The door opened only a little. Something on the other side was blocking it. I put my hand through the gap and felt on the floor.

And my hand felt something made of cloth. Then, as I moved my hand around, I felt something dry and bumpy. It was a hand!

I almost jumped out of my sneakers. A body! I was about to run off for help, but the dog barked with excitement and tried to squeeze through the opening.

It couldn't get through, so it ran around the front of the house and leaped back through the window.

I probably should have gone home and gotten Mom right then. Instead, I followed the dog through the window, making sure I didn't catch myself on anything that would cut me.

The inside of the house looked like a dumpster. There were piles of old newspapers. Bottles lay on the floor. Cans and rags spilled out of cardboard boxes. Cobwebs hung from the lampshades. The house smelled moldy, as if the doors and windows had been kept shut for years.

Then I had a scary thought. What if the smell came from something dead? It made my palms sweat as if I was watching a horror movie!

The dog whined. It wanted me to go further inside. I didn't want to go. I stuck my head around the doorway very, very slowly.

I stepped into the hallway and, as I turned the corner toward the front door, I saw more and more. First a slipper. Then a bare foot. Then a leg, dressed in pajamas. Then a another leg, twisted underneath the top leg. Then arms and a body.

Then I saw an old man's face, with straggly hair and a wispy beard. He made kind of a groaning noise and opened his eyes. He looked as though he didn't know where he was.

He seemed to be trying to say something, but couldn't. He lifted his hand up weakly and pointed at me. For an instant, I thought he was accusing me of something, but then the dog ran up to him and started to lick his face. That's when the old man smiled.

I hadn't realized it before, but I was too concerned to be afraid.

Chapter Four
Emergency

It had to be Mr. Shaw. No one else
would be wearing pajamas at number
nine. He didn't look bad-tempered, or
like a burglar or a mad scientist—and he
wasn't dead.

That's when I saw why the door

wouldn't open any farther. Mr. Shaw was lying against it.

When the dog licked him, he groaned. He pulled himself to sit up, struggling.

"Are you all right?" I said.

As soon as I said it, I thought it was a stupid thing to say. I mean, you don't lie on the floor if you're feeling OK!

Mr. Shaw gasped. Somehow, I understood that he wanted water.

I ran to the kitchen and opened cupboards until I found a glass. Then I filled it from the faucet.

I had to hold the glass for Mr. Shaw. He took a few sips of water and then slumped to the floor. I picked up the phone to call 9-1-1, but the phone didn't work.

"Hold on, Mr. Shaw!" I said.

I took off for home—carefully through

the window—and dialed 9-1-1. I told them my name and where Mr. Shaw was, and that I didn't know exactly what was wrong with him.

Then I grabbed Mom by the hand and ran back to Mr. Shaw's house.

"Where on Earth are we going, Troy?" she asked.

"Mr. Shaw's in trouble!" I shouted.

The front door was wide open. Mr. Shaw was still on the floor, and the dog was licking his hand.

"Phew," said Mom, when she saw the house. She wrinkled her nose. "What a pigsty!"

We looked after Mr. Shaw until the ambulance arrived.

Mom gave him lots of water. She said not to move him, in case his back was hurt.

In a shaky voice, Mr. Shaw told us what happened.

He was trying to move some furniture, but he had a nasty fall. He thought his leg was broken. He managed to crawl to the fireplace and light a fire to get people's attention. When that didn't work, he crawled to the front door to try to open it. But he was too weak to stand up.

I realized that if the dog hadn't jumped out the window after me, Mr. Shaw would have died.

When the ambulance came, the paramedics put Mr. Shaw on a stretcher. They did it carefully, but he still groaned.

The dog licked him and whined.

"My dog," moaned Mr. Shaw. "Don't forget my dog."

"No dogs allowed at the hospital," said the driver. "Sorry."

The ambulance drove off, with Mr. Shaw inside and the dog sitting at our feet, whining softly.

Chapter Five
Lucky

A short while later, number nine went up for sale. A new family with a boy about my age moved in there.

They cleaned it up and gave it a fresh coat of paint. It looks like a different house now.

Mom and I sometimes visit Mr. Shaw in his retirement home. People can look after him now, and move his furniture for him if he wants.

He likes to see us—and Lucky.

Lucky is his dog.

They don't allow dogs at the retirement home, so Lucky is staying with us now. He's a great dog. He makes me think of the day he helped to save Mr. Shaw's life. That makes me feel good.

I call him Lucky because Mom said he's lucky she agreed to let me keep him!